MĀORI MADE EASY POCKET GUIDE

Professor Scotty Morrison (Ngāti Whakaue) is the well-known presenter of current affairs programmes *Te Karere* and *Marae*. He holds a Master's degree (Education), is working towards his PhD, and has been an Adjunct Professor and the Director of Māori Student and Community Engagement at Auckland's Unitec Institute of Technology. In 2017, he was appointed to a new role at Massey University's Te Pūtahi-a-Toi (School of Māori Art, Knowledge and Education), working alongside his wife Stacey in a strategic, advocacy and lecturing capacity.

In 2019, Scotty was awarded the inaugural Te Tohu Kōrurenga Hau Culture Change award by Te Taura Whiri i te Reo Māori/the Māori Language Commission for his leadership and innovation as a teacher of te reo Māori.

Scotty lives in Tāmaki Makaurau with Stacey and their three children, Hawaiki, Kurawa

MĀORI MADE EASY POCKET GUIDE

Essential greetings, phrases and tikanga for every day

Scotty Morrison

PENGUIN BOOKS

CONTENTS

KUPU WHAKATAKI
INTRODUCTION

Kia ora anō koutou katoa and welcome to the *Māori Made Easy Pocket Guide* – a book designed to be at your side everywhere you go, to help you use te reo Māori in the various situations and contexts you encounter each and every day!

Over the past few years especially, I have been inundated by all sorts of people eager to learn the Māori language and more about the country we live in. I am very aware however, that we are all busy and often don't have the time or ability to actively learn te reo Māori – even if we want to! Don't worry, e hoa mā – I'm here to help.

The thinking behind the *Māori Made Easy Pocket Guide* is to provide, in a clear and simple way, language and know-how that you can use, not necessarily learn. It's your one-stop shop, your go-to handbook for the basics of te reo Māori.

It represents a careful selection of some of the best and

most usable content from my previous books, updated and reworked for this new kaupapa, and supported by brand-new, made-to-measure material, too.

The first section – Te Reo Māori – obviously enough, provides ready-to-use words and phrases for most arenas of everyday life, as well as a few history and culture lessons along the way, and hints and tips to give you a good headstart.

The second section – Te Ao Māori – gives you a lot of important background knowledge for many aspects of the Māori world and ways of being; that is, the foundation for the language.

You get easy access to sentence structures, phrases, colloquialisms and proverbs you can use when doing things like socialising, playing sport, talking on the phone, driving in the car or composing an email. There are also updated sections on cultural aspects like Matariki, tikanga Māori during meetings, what to expect when participating in a traditional pōwhiri, and how to use pepeha, for both Māori and non-Māori.

I've tried to keep things dynamic and varied – you'll find that some chapters are largely lists of handy phrases, others offer the same alongside more context and commentary, with others going a little deeper into matters of tikanga, mātauranga Māori and history, especially in the Te Ao Māori section.

Start with small things, like a word you use on a daily

basis that you switch out for the Māori equivalent, a phrase you are going to use every day, or a whakataukī that will become your mantra for the month ahead. You can also analyse some of the principles contained within the tikanga discussed in this book and use those same principles to guide you and your family towards positive change.

I don't expect anyone to read this book from start to finish – but that being said, be my guest! Dip in, dip out. Take what you need and take te reo to the world. You'll never regret it, I promise. Thank you for embracing our beautiful language in whatever way might suit your life.

HE HĪTORIA MŌ TE REO MĀORI
A HISTORY OF THE MĀORI LANGUAGE

Aotearoa New Zealand and its indigenous Māori language have had a tumultuous and colourful history with all the drama and passion you want for any good story. This offers insight into why the language is in the state of peril it is today, and what the critical factors are for its future.

Māori language is a close relation of the languages spoken in the Cook Islands, Tahiti, Rapanui, Marquesas and Hawai'i. So close, in fact, that I like to tell my students that when you learn Māori, you are actually learning many other Eastern Pacific languages at the same time! According to most accounts, it was about 1000 or so years ago when the Māori ancestors made their monumental excursion across the expansive ocean to Aotearoa New Zealand. There are many theories about the evolution of the Māori language, but most historians and language experts agree that the ancestors immediately had to adapt their language to a new environment in Aotearoa New Zealand. There were new species of animal life, new weather patterns and new economic activities that led to the development of new names and words. This was the birth of the Māori language we know today.

Māori were, and still are, fiercely tribal, and upholding the authority over their lands and assets sometimes led to conflict. This could be settled by conquest, mediation or traditional customs, such as a union between high-ranking members of each tribe. Dialectal differences emerged because of the distance that some of these early ancestors lived apart from each other and the differences in their surroundings. Most Māori language experts are of the opinion that these dialectal differences did not affect their ability to communicate with each other and this is still the case in today's society.

Māori language and culture remained the status quo even though missionaries had arrived in the early part of the 1800s, bringing with them new philosophies and ideologies based on the word of God. These clergymen introduced Māori to written language by translating parts of the Bible into te reo Māori. Early missionaries, such as Samuel Marsden, made the first attempts to write down the Māori language in 1814.

In August 1839, the British Government sent Captain William Hobson (one of my ancestors on my Pākehā side!) out to Aotearoa New Zealand as British consul, with orders to annex part or all of the country and place it under British rule. Part of his mission to acquire the sovereignty of Aotearoa New Zealand was to sign a treaty with the native Māori chiefs. The British Government could see that the situation in New Zealand was heading downhill fast and wanted to establish sovereignty as soon as possible. Hobson had a deadline.

At 4 p.m. on 4 February 1840, Hobson gave the final draft of the treaty to Henry Williams to translate into the Māori language. Williams was head of the Church Missionary Society and had been a missionary in Aotearoa New Zealand since 1823. Now we're talking about a serious deadline. Helped by his son Edward, the translation was finished by Williams before 10 a.m. the next day. However, any translator will tell you that was a very short timeframe for such a critical job – and he didn't even have Microsoft Word!

As a result, some of the words used to translate important concepts contained in the treaty have been the subject of vigorous debate ever since. As the chiefs started arriving at Waitangi, Hobson, Williams and Busby met behind locked doors to check and finalise the accuracy of the treaty. At this last moment, before the treaty was presented to the chiefs, Busby asked to substitute one crucial word of the

Māori text. The translation of *sovereignty* had been *mana motuhake* but Busby changed it to *kāwanatanga*.

Māori language experts are generally unified in the belief that had *mana motuhake* remained in the treaty to describe the cession of sovereignty to the British and their monarchy, the treaty itself may have been rejected by the Māori chiefs gathered at Waitangi that day. *Mana motuhake* is in fact a more adept and accurate description of *sovereignty* than *kāwanatanga*. According to the *New Zealand Oxford Dictionary*, *sovereignty* is 'supreme power or complete authority'. *Mana motuhake*, in Māori terms, describes that concept. *Kāwanatanga* describes a much softer form of rule that could be accurately translated as 'governorship'.

By the early 1860s, Europeans and the English language had become dominant in Aotearoa New Zealand, with Māori language starting to retreat to Māori communities in remote areas that existed away from the European majority. Te reo Māori was now officially being discouraged and many Māori themselves began to question its relevance in a European-dominated world where the most important value seemed to be to get ahead as an individual, which was in contrast to traditional Māori values of working for the collective and focusing on whānau and community-based goals. Acts of legislation were created by the government to assimilate Māori into the 'civilised' European lifestyle and to destroy the Māori language. The Native Schools Act of

1858 stated that 'Schools would assist in the process of assimilation'.

In 1871, the government ruled that all instruction in native schools had to be in the English language, effectively shutting down Māori language in schools. Following this move from the government, Māori children were physically beaten and made to eat soap if they were caught speaking their language in the school grounds. A prominent Māori leader and politician, Sir James Henare, remembered being sent into the bush to cut a piece of supplejack vine with which he was struck for speaking te reo Māori in the school grounds. Apparently, one teacher told him that, 'English is the bread and butter language, and if you want to earn your bread and butter you must speak English'.

Despite the legislation put in place to nullify the Māori language, its flame still burnt reasonably brightly until the arrival of World War Two. Many of our young Māori men, the next generation of speakers on our marae and leaders in our communities, enlisted to fight overseas and were lost. This had a detrimental effect on the intergenerational transmission of the language in Māori homes. Add to this the urban shift of the 1960s and 1970s and, all of a sudden, Māori language was on the endangered species list.

From the 1970s, many Māori people reasserted their identity, with the revival of the language an integral part of the renaissance. New groups emerged and made a commitment to strengthening Māori culture and the language. Two of these groups, Ngā Tamatoa (The Young Warriors) represented by the late Hana Te Hemara, and the Te Reo Māori Society, represented by Lee Smith, delivered a 30,000-signature petition to Parliament on 14 September 1972 requesting government support to promote the language. This eventually led to the establishment of Māori Language Day, and subsequently Māori Language Week, which is still celebrated today.

The 1970s really was crunch time for te reo Māori and was in fact a period of tremendous political change for Māori in Aotearoa New Zealand. Race relations came to a head with the Māori Land March/Hīkoi of 1975, which galvanised Māori into action. In the same year, the Waitangi Tribunal was established by the government to hear Māori grievances with regard to the Treaty of Waitangi and to make recommendations of compensation to the Crown. Also in 1975, a language revival plan called Whakatupuranga Rua Mano with a 25-year horizon was implemented by the tribal confederation of Te Ātiawa, Ngāti Raukawa and Ngāti Toa Rangatira. At that time, they had no one under the age of 30 who could converse in the Māori language. Today, according to their statistics, there are approximately 700–800 descendants under the age of 30 who can speak the language, as a result of those revival plans being followed through to fruition.

It's here that I'd like to mention a man named Dun Mihaka, described as a 'Māori publicity seeker' by the

Truth newspaper in 1971 and a 'Māori land activist' by the Palmerston North *Tribune* in 1979. Over several years, between 1975 and 1979, he tested the courts of this country in different ways to ascertain whether the Māori language had any real status in the constitutional framework of Aotearoa New Zealand. In one case he was involved in, he staunchly refused to accept the court's jurisdiction over him unless he was allowed, by right of the Treaty of Waitangi, to address the court in the Māori language. That dispute went from the district court to the high court and eventually to the court of appeal. While Mr Mihaka lost this argument, his actions set the tone for the next wave of opposition: 'E te Kāwanatanga, ka ahatia e koe te reo Māori e mate haere nei?' 'Government, what are you going to do about the plight of the Māori language?'

The Māori language renaissance continued in 1978 with the creation of Aotearoa New Zealand's first official bilingual school in Rūātoki. Kāterina Te Heikōkō Mataira and Ngoingoi Pēwhairangi launched a community-based language learning programme in 1979, where native speakers of Māori were trained to be tutors. Called Te Ataarangi, this programme utilised coloured rods and large amounts of spoken language to teach elementary level Māori language.

In 1981, the first kōhanga reo or Māori-language preschool opened at Pukeatua Marae in Wainuiomata. Kōhanga reo were the result of a major conference about the language in

Wellington in 1980. The elders who attended the conference called for a fresh approach to stabilise the language once and for all, 'Where babies could be fed on the milk of their language from birth.'

Efforts to secure the survival of Māori language went to another level in 1985 when a grievance about the treatment of the Māori language was lodged with the Waitangi Tribunal. The claim made in relation to the language was the first one initiated for an intangible asset or taonga.

This word 'taonga', meaning treasure, occurs in article two of the Treaty of Waitangi, where Māori are guaranteed protection of all their taonga. Māori considered their language a taonga. The Waitangi Tribunal found the Treaty of Waitangi was 'directed to ensuring a place for two peoples in Aotearoa New Zealand'. It questioned whether the promise of the treaty could be achieved 'if there is not a recognised place for the language of one of the partners to the Treaty'.

There were various arguments against the claim from European New Zealanders, with some saying that minority languages should not be imposed on the majority, that the Māori language could not adapt to the modern world, that it was not an international language and that official recognition was an empty gesture. The tribunal pointed out that with official recognition, minority languages had survived and flourished elsewhere. Official recognition of both languages and cultures would encourage respect for their differences.

The tribunal released its findings in 1986, recommending five ways for the government to remedy breaches of the treaty regarding the Māori language:

- Pass laws allowing te reo Māori to be used in courts and dealings with local and central government.
- Establish a statutory body to 'supervise and foster the use of Māori language'.
- Examine the teaching of te reo Māori and 'ensure that all children who wish to learn Māori should be able to do so'.
- Recognise and protect te reo in broadcasting.
- Ensure that speaking both Māori and English be a necessary or desirable requirement for certain public service positions.

In 1987, the Māori Language Act was passed, establishing the Māori language as an official language of Aotearoa New Zealand and conferring the right to speak Māori in legal proceedings regardless of ability to understand or communicate in English, or any other language. It also established Te Taura Whiri i te Reo Māori / the Māori Language Commission. This legislation forced the government to acknowledge that it had a responsibility to ensure the language's survival and of course provide funding.

Over the past few years, te reo Māori has enjoyed an increased presence on television, on radio and in schools. There is a dedicated Māori television station, which has a mandate to revive and retain the Māori language, and also a dedicated entity called Te Mātāwai, which is responsible for language revitalisation in the whānau, the hapū, the iwi and the community. However, for te reo Māori to thrive it needs to be spoken, and spoken widely, before we can say it is truly back from the brink.

New data from the 2021 General Social Survey (GSS), collected between April and August 2021, showed that the ability of New Zealanders (aged 15 and over) to speak te reo Māori in day-to-day conversation has improved.

Since 2018, the proportion of people able to speak more than a few words or phrases of te reo Māori rose from 24 per cent to 30 per cent. The proportion of people able to speak te reo Māori at least fairly well also increased, from 6.1 per cent in 2018 to 7.9 per cent in 2021. These are encouraging statistics, but there is still a lot to be done to ensure the continued health of the language.

One of the advantages te reo Māori has is that it is a language that moves with the times. As society changes and new technology arises, te reo Māori adapts! We take selfies or kiriāhua on our phone. AI is a new phenomenon we call in Māori atamai hangahanga. These words are crafted and created using old words to create new ones and the fascinating thing is that the Māori words tell you what the actual function of the new item is, for example, kiri = skin, āhua = appearance, which could translate to 'me in my own skin' or 'selfie'!

I hope this summary has opened your eyes and your heart to the story of te reo Māori, a language that has had to fight hard for its very survival. The future is now in our hands. When you begin to utter the phrases and words in this book, you will be contributing to the renaissance of a language that is over 1000 years old. I believe Māori language can offer something to all of us.

So, kia kaha koe, e hoa, give it heaps and thank you for your contribution!

TE REO MĀORI

THE MĀORI LANGUAGE

WHAKAHUA
PRONUNCIATION

Māori is a phonetic language that, when compared with other languages of the world, is reasonably simple to pronounce. All that is required is a bit of attention, a dose of respect, and a sprinkle of patience. The key to correct pronunciation is to master the sounds of the five vowels: *a, e, i, o, u*. The best way for most people to learn the vowel sounds is by using examples in English.

The vowel **a** is pronounced as in the English c<u>u</u>t
The vowel **e** is pronounced as in the English <u>e</u>gg
The vowel **i** is pronounced as in the English k<u>ey</u>
The vowel **o** is pronounced as in the English p<u>aw</u>
The vowel **u** is pronounced as in the English sh<u>oe</u>

There are long and short vowel sounds, with macrons used on the long vowels to indicate the long vowel sound.

The vowel **ā** is pronounced as in the English c<u>a</u>r
The vowel **ē** is pronounced as in the English p<u>ea</u>r
The vowel **ī** is pronounced as in the English <u>ee</u>l
The vowel **ō** is pronounced as in the English p<u>ou</u>r
The vowel **ū** is pronounced as in the English r<u>oo</u>f

If you give the wrong sound to these vowels, you'll most likely mess up the correct pronunciation of a Māori name or word.

The words *Taranaki* and *Waikato*, for example, are commonly mispronounced because the sound of the vowel *a* is said flat like you might hear in the word *cat*. Sometimes, long vowel sounds are shortened or short vowel sounds are lengthened, which gives the word a whole new meaning. The most obvious example of this is the word *mana*, which translates to *power, authority, control, influence*. As you can see by the way it is written, there are no macrons on the two vowels in *mana*, and yet, even in broadcasting, people tend to assign a macron to the first *a* so it gets mispronounced as *māna*, which is a word denoting possession and translates to *for him/her*. Once you've got the hang of correct pronunciation of the vowel sounds, it should give you the confidence to dive on in there and make an honest attempt to say any Māori word correctly because, apart from length, the pronunciation of each vowel in Māori words is constant.

There are 10 consonants: *h, k, m, n, p, r, t, w, ng, wh*. The pronunciation of these consonants is pretty straight-forward and they are generally pronounced as they are in English, but most people have some difficulty with the *ng* combination. The *ng* is said as it sounds in the English word *singer*. A common mistake is to pronounce it as it appears in the word *finger*, with a hard 'g'. The *wh* combination is usually pronounced as an English *f* sound, except in the Taranaki region, where it is omitted for a soft inaudible 'h'. The word *Whanganui* is written with an *h* in it, but a speaker from the area will say it like this: *Wanganui*. The *r* is rolled. It almost sounds similar to a *d* in English, but softer, like the *d* in the word *shudder*.

The final consonant that may differ slightly from English pronunciation is the *t*. The pronunciation of this consonant varies depending on which vowel appears after it. When followed by an *i* or *u* it has an *s* sound, but it's not nearly as prominent as the *s* sound you hear in English. When followed by an *a*, *e* or *o*, it's pronounced *t* with little or no *s* sound.

MITA
DIALECTS

The major differences in terms of language style pertaining to the tribes of Aotearoa New Zealand are found in the pronunciation of words, the vocabulary and the idioms.

Some linguists assert the theory that older speakers of Māori are more likely to speak Māori identifiable with a particular dialect or region, whereas younger speakers of Māori tend to do a lot of dialect mixing, especially those living in urban areas. This view does have some merit, with the onus being on the young people to rediscover their own particular dialect if they are not living in their tribal regions. The majority of young Māori speakers are outside their own tribal areas, being taught by people who speak a dialect that is not their own. I remember my Māori language lecturer at Waikato University, who was from the Tūhoe tribe in the eastern Bay of Plenty region, telling me I was sounding like a Tūhoe, even though I am from the Te Arawa confederation of tribes in the Rotorua area. My main focus at that stage was just to learn the language; dialect was irrelevant. If you are fortunate enough to be learning your own dialect, great! If you're not, don't worry! It's possible to learn your dialect at a later stage, and anyway, in my opinion, the differences are not huge. To illustrate this point, let's take a look at some examples.

In the Whanganui and Taranaki regions of the North Island, the *h* is not pronounced and is replaced instead by a soft inaudible *h*, so the word *whenua* (land) becomes *wenua*, and *whakarongo* (listen) becomes *wakarongo*.

If we cross over to the northeast of the North Island to the Tūhoe region in the eastern Bay of Plenty, *ng* has merged with *n*, so the word *kanga* (to curse) sounds like *kana*, and *tangihanga* (funeral) sounds like *tanihana*. In the South Island dialects, the *ng* diphthong is a *k*, so you get words like *karanga* (to call) with the *ng* replaced by a *k* to become *karaka*. North Island tribes call the highest peak of the South Island *Aorangi* (Mt Cook), but to local tribes of the South Island it's *Aoraki*.

The Ngāti Porou tribe on the East Coast of the North Island has a well-known colloquialism, *Ka mau te wehi*, meaning 'awesome'. The Ngāpuhi people who inhabit the Kaikohe region have a similar colloquialism which is just as well known, *Haramai tētahi āhua*. If you were to venture to Te Tai Rawhiti you may be greeted by the local people with a *Kai te aha?* For most tribal groups *Kei te aha?* means 'What are you doing?' but on the East Coast it's a form of greeting which is saying, 'Hello, how are you?' You may have recognised the difference in spelling of the *kai* and the *kei* in these examples, which again is a characteristic of dialectal difference.

My advice to you is to not get too caught up in the dialect debate. At the end of the day, the differences in te reo Māori are probably not even big enough to be termed 'dialectal'. Regional variations may be a more accurate term to describe them at present. Just remember, there is only one Māori language with many dialects, so it doesn't matter which dialect you are learning, the outcome will be the same, the ability to speak Māori!

HE MIHI
GREETINGS

Greeting others in a meaningful way is very important in Māori culture. It means choosing the appropriate language and sometimes performing the traditional pressing of noses or the *hongi*.

The hongi has become more and more commonplace among our communities in Aotearoa New Zealand. It is our own unique way of greeting someone, so I say embrace it and use it – but with respect. It is a very significant and sacred act, so understanding about where it comes from and what it means is required.

When Māori greet each other by pressing noses, the tradition of sharing the *hā* or breath of life is considered to have come directly from the gods. When performing the hongi, you are paying homage to the creation of the first human (according to Māori folklore, this is Hineahuone) and all her descendants. You are also paying homage to the descent lines of the person you are performing the hongi with. The breath of life is exchanged and intermingled.

Let's now look at some basic greetings of 'Hello' and 'How are you?' to initiate a conversation.

Kia ora.
Hello.

Kei te pēhea koe?
How are you?

Kei te pai.
Good.

A koe?
And you?

Kei te harikoa au.
I am happy.

Kei te ngenge au.
I am tired.

Kei te maremare au.
I have a bit of a cold.

Ka kite anō.
See you later.

Hei te wā.
Catch you up.

Ngā manaakitanga.
All the best.

I have complete confidence in your ability to speak Māori and use these phrases correctly, but there may be times when you don't understand what is being said to you. Here are some tools to help you overcome the language barrier.

He aha?
What?

Homai anō.
Give me that again.

He aha te tikanga o tēnā kōrero?
What does that mean?

Ko wai? / A wai?
Who?

He aha te kupu Māori mō . . . ?
What's the Māori word for . . . ?

Kia kaha ake tō reo.
Please speak louder.

Kāore au i te rongo.
I can't hear.

Kāore au i rongo i tēnā.
I didn't hear that.

Kāore au i te mārama.
I don't understand.

Kia āta kōrero.
(Please) speak more slowly.

Kōrero mai anō.
(Please) say that again.

Tauria mai tēnā kupu.
(Please) spell that out.

Me pēhea taku kī . . . ?
How do I say . . . ?

E mōhio ana koe ki te kōrero Pākehā?
Can you speak English?

He pai ake tōku reo Pākehā i tōku reo Māori.
I speak English better than Māori.

And now, a few more questions and other interactions to get to know each other a little better.

Ko wai tō ingoa?
What's your name?

Ko . . . tōku ingoa.
My name is . . .

Nō hea koe?
Where are you from?

Nō tāwāhi au.
I'm from overseas.

Nō Whangārei au.
I'm from Whangārei.

He pai te tūtaki ki a koe!
I'm pleased to meet you!

Ko taku . . . tēnei.
This is my . . .

hoa rangatira	*partner, spouse.*
hoa wahine	*wife.*
hoa tāne	*husband.*
tamaiti	*child.*
tama	*son.*
tamāhine	*daughter.*
hoa	*friend.*
whaiāipo	*partner, spouse, boyfriend, girlfriend, husband, wife.*

Ko aku . . . ēnei.
These are my . . .

tamariki	*children.*
tama	*sons.*
tamāhine	*daughters.*
hoa	*friends.*

Kei te pēhea tō . . . ?
How is your . . .

whānau?	*family?*
māmā?	*mother?*
pāpā?	*father?*
tuakana?	*older brother (of male)?*
tuakana?	*older sister (of female)?*
teina?	*younger brother (of male)?*
teina?	*younger sister (of female)?*
tuahine?	*sister (of male)?*
tungāne?	*brother (of female)?*
whanaunga?	*cousin?*
irāmutu?	*niece/nephew?*
taumau?	*fiancée/fiancé?*
kiritata?	*neighbour?*
rangatira?	*boss/leader?*

Kei te pēhea ō . . . ?
How are your . . .

tamariki?	*children?*
mātua?	*parents?*
kaumātua?	*grandparents?*

E hia ō tau?
How old are you?

Rangatahi tonu koe.
You're still young.

Rangatahi rawa atu koe i a au.
You're way younger than me.

He aha tāu i haere mai ai ki konei?
What brings you here?

He aha tō mahi i konei?
What brings you here?

He mahi pakihi.
Business (brings me here).

He whakatā noa iho.
Just on holiday.

He hiahia tōku kia kite i tēnei whenua rerehua.
I wanted to see this beautiful country.

He hoa ōku kei konei.
I have friends here.

E hia te roa o tō noho?
How long are you staying?

Kei te mārena koe?
Are you married?

Kei te mārena au.
I am married.

Kei te takakau au.
I am single.

Kei te noho tahi māua ko taku whaiāipo.
I live with my boyfriend/girlfriend.

Kua tokorau.
I am divorced.

He pouaru au.
I am a widow.

He ātaahua ō tamariki.
You have beautiful children.

HE POROTAU
FAREWELLS

Learning how to say hello and goodbye in a new language is usually one of the first things someone will begin with when attempting to speak that language. The greeting 'Kia ora' has been normalised so much here in Aotearoa – in my opinion, based on the extensive travel I do around the country and among our communities, it has become the preferred greeting of what must be half the population. I also think some of our farewells are approaching that mark in terms of their usage in everyday contexts. It's fantastic to hear greetings and farewells becoming such a natural part of how we talk to each other – and they are definitely something you can learn quickly and put into practice pretty much straight away. So, give it a go e hoa mā! Here are examples of common farewells to get you started.

Ka kite anō.
See you again.

Kia pai te rā.
Have a nice day.

Kia hua nui te rā.
Have a brilliant day.

Haere rā.
Goodbye (to someone leaving).

E noho rā.
Goodbye (to someone staying).

Hei konā.
See you later.

Hei te wā.
Catch you up.

Hei ākuanei.
See you soon.

Hei te ata.
See you in the morning.

Hei te ahiahi nei.
See you this afternoon.

Hei te pō nei.
See you tonight.

Hei āpōpō.
See you tomorrow.

Hei te Mane.
See you on Monday.

Hei te Tūrei.
See you on Tuesday.

Hei te Wenerei.
See you on Wednesday.

Hei te Tāite.
See you on Thursday.

Hei te Paraire.
See you on Friday.

Hei te Rāhoroi.
See you on Saturday.

Hei te Rātapu.
See you on Sunday.

Hei tērā wiki.
See you next week.

Hei tērā marama.
See you next month.

Hei tērā tau.
See you next year.

And now, a few things to say when you know the conversation or the time you are spending with someone is coming to an end – some phrases you may use before you say goodbye.

Hēoi anō.
Oh well.

Me haere au.
I had better go.

I pai tēnei noho tahi.
This was a great get-together.

Ka nui tēnei.
This is enough/sufficient.

Me tuku au i a koe.
I should let you go now.

Me waiho koe e au.
I should leave you now.

Ka tukuna koe ināianei.
I'll let you go now. / I'll leave you to it.

Kāti.
That'll do.

Kua eke te wā.
Time to go.

Kua tae mai te wā.
The time has arrived.

Kua pau te wā.
The time is up.

Me mutu taku whakahōhā i a koe.
I'll stop bugging you now.

Kua pai tēnei hui.
This has been a good meeting/get-together.

NGĀ ĪMĒRA ME NGĀ RETA
EMAILS AND LETTERS

As technology advances, writing letters has become more and more obsolete. However, there are still some fundamentals you may wish to include when writing a letter, an email, or even a text message to someone. Te Taura Whiri i te Reo Maori/the Māori Language Commission has stipulated that when writing the date, it should look like this:

19 November 1970, or: Te 19 o Whiringa-a-rangi / Noema 1970

However, most people I know will shorten this down to the following.

19 Whiringa-a-rangi / Noema 1970

You may want to use the first example if the letter or email is more formal; the second could be used in less formal communication.

Once we have written the correct date, we can then move on to some opening greetings. Choosing the appropriate language is important and shows respect between the people who are engaging with or meeting each other for the first time. *Tēnā koe* is considered a more formal way of greeting one person, so you could start your formal email or letter with:

Tēnā koe	*Dear Sir/Madam*
or:	
E te rangatira, tēnā koe	*Dear Sir/Madam*
Tēnā koe, e te rangatira	*Dear Sir/Madam*

The word *rangatira* denotes a high-ranking person or someone you have respect for as having chiefly qualities. It is not gender-specific, so can be used to address a woman, man or takatāpui person.

Now, you may have noticed that the *tēnā koe* greeting is used for one person only. There are two basic greetings when addressing one person: *kia ora* and *tēnā koe*. Both of these greetings are widely known in Aotearoa New Zealand. *Kia ora*, however, is considered by many to be a little less formal than *tēnā koe*.

Keep in mind that these will change depending on how

many people you are talking to. If you are greeting two people, use the personal pronoun *kōrua*, which means *you two*: 'Kia ora kōrua' or 'Tēnā kōrua'. If you are greeting three or more people, use *koutou*: 'Kia ora koutou' or 'Tēnā koutou'. So a formal greeting to two people will look like this:

Tēnā kōrua, or: E ngā rangatira, tēnā kōrua

And a formal greeting to three or more people will look like this:

Tēnā koutou, or: E ngā rangatira, tēnā koutou

Terms of address are frequently used instead of names. These terms are probably more appropriate when you know the person or when a more informal style of communication is being used. Some of the most common terms of address are:

Tēnā koe, e hoa – *used for a friend*
Tēnā koe, e kare – *used for an intimate friend*
Tēnā koe, e tama – *used for a boy or young man*
Tēnā koe, e hine – *used for a girl or young woman*
Tēnā koe, e koro – *used for an elderly man*
Tēnā koe, e kui – *used for an elderly woman*
Tēnā koe, e tā – *used in a similar way to 'sir' in English*
Tēnā koe, e te kahurangi – *used in a similar way to 'madam' in English*

Tēnā koe can be replaced by *kia ora* for a more informal greeting, and if you are talking to two or more people add *mā* to the end to show the plural:

Kia ora, e hoa mā – *used for a bunch of friends*
Kia ora, e kare mā – *used for a bunch of intimate friends*
Kia ora, e tama mā – *used for a group of boys or young men*
Kia ora, e hine mā – *used for a group of girls or young women*
Kia ora, e koro mā – *used for a group of elderly men*
Kia ora, e kui mā – *used for a group of elderly women*
Kia ora, e tā mā – *used for a group of high-ranking men*
Kia ora, kahurangi mā – *used for a group of high-ranking women*

The age of the speaker and the person being addressed will influence which term is used. The word *mā* should be used if more than one person is being addressed, but not when the function words *te* or *ngā* are present, as in the greeting 'e te rangatira'. Personal names can also be used when greeting, but note: if the name is a short one with only one long or two short vowels, it is preceded by *e*: 'Tēnā koe, e Hone' or 'Kia ora, e Pita'. If it's longer, or not a Māori name, the *e* is disregarded: 'Kia ora Te Ururoa', 'Tēnā koe Tariana', 'Tēnā koe William', or 'Kia ora Joe'.

Below are some other opening addresses you can use in a group email, or to a large group of people. The translations may sound unnatural but this is just a reflection of cultural difference.

E ngā hau e whā, tēnā koutou katoa.
To all of the four winds, I greet you all.

E ngā mana, e ngā reo, tēnā koutou katoa.
To all authorities and voices, I greet you all.

E ngā karangatanga maha, tēnā koutou katoa.
To all the affiliations, I greet you all.

E ngā iwi katoa, tēnā koutou katoa.
To all people and tribes, I greet you all.

E ngā mātāwaka, tēnā koutou katoa.
To all throughout this place, I greet you all.

Kei aku nui, kei aku rahi, tēnā koutou katoa.
To my esteemed colleagues, I greet you all.

Sometimes, during formal written communication, after your initial greeting, it is entirely appropriate to include a reference and acknowledgement to those who have passed on. This practice may be unfamiliar to many people but it is a reflection of Māori spirituality and the constant connection with ancestors in *te ao wairua* or the spiritual realm, and is commonplace when Māori are writing to each other. Our ancestors are always considered to be with us and available to be called on at any time. This is why during formal speechmaking or *whaikōrero*, or even in this context of formal written communication via email or letter, a *poroporoaki* or words of farewell and acknowledgement to the deceased are offered.

The inclusion of this part of your communication will be your personal choice, and may depend on a number of factors, e.g. who you are writing to, how well you know the person, and the content or reason for the communication. Just like your opening greeting, there are many ways of expressing this sentiment. Here are a few examples.

1. E ngā mate o te wā, haere, haere, haere atu rā.
To those who have passed on, I farewell you all.

2. E ngā pare raukura o te mate, haere, haere, haere atu rā.
To our precious loved ones who are no longer with us, I farewell you all.

3. Ki ngā raukura kua maunu atu ki moana uriuri, haere, haere, haere atu rā.
To the sacred plumes who have drifted off to the depths of the wide ocean, I farewell you all.

4. Ko te ua i te rangi, ko te ua i aku kamo. E ngā tini aituā o tēnā iwi, o tēnā iwi, haere atu rā koutou ki te pūtahitanga o Rehua, ki te kāpunipunitanga o te wairua.
My tears flow like rain from the sky above. To our loved ones who have passed on, I pay homage to you all as you reside in the highest of the heavens, the gathering place of the spirits.

5. E te tipua, e Whiro, tēnei te whakatau atu. E ngā mate huhua o te wā o nāianei, o te wā kua hipa, tangi hotuhotu ana te ngākau, tangi apakura ana te manawa ki a koutou kua ngaro i te rā nei. Ngā rau tīpare o te iwi, ngā huia kaimanawa o te tangata, tau mai rā. E kore koutou e wareware i a mātou.

To Whiro, the deity of death and calamity, I pay acknowledgement. To all the deceased, of recent times and times past, the heart still weeps and laments at your absence. Our illustrious ones, our precious ones, rest in peace. You will never be forgotten.

If you are going to include a poroporoaki in your correspondence, make sure you end with one of the following lines to bring the sentiment of your words back from the spiritual realm and the dwelling place of the deceased to the realm of the living, creating balance and normality again before you begin with the reason or business of your email or letter.

1. Hoki rawa mai ki a tātou, tēnā anō tātou katoa.
I now return back to us, and once again greet us all.

2. Ko rātou ki a rātou, ko tātou ki a tātou, tēnā anō tātou katoa.
Let the spirits reside in the spirit world, and to us here in the physical world, greetings again to us all.

3. Nō reira, ko te pito mate ki te pito mate, ko te pito ora ki te pito ora, tēnā anō tātou katoa.
And so, let the deceased rest in peace, and the living keep on living, greetings again to us all.

4. Kua ea te wāhi ki a rātou, ka hoki mai ki a tātou, te hunga ora, tēnā anō rā tātou katoa.
The deceased have been acknowledged, I now return to us, the living descendants, greetings once again.

5. Ko te akaaka o te rangi ki a rātou, ko te akaaka o te whenua ki a tātou, tēnā anō rā tātou katoa.
The connector to the heavens remains with those who have passed, the connector to the land remains with us, and so I greet us all once again.

Now, to conclude your email or letter, we can use some of these as our *kupu whakamutunga* or *kupu whakatepe*, closing remarks.

1. Me mutu pea i konei. Ngā mihi nui. Nā (ingoa).
Enough said. Thank you for your time. From (name).

2. Kua rahi tēnei. Ngā manaakitanga o te wā. Nāku, nā (ingoa).
Enough said. All the best. Yours faithfully, (name).

3. Kāti ake i konei. Noho ora mai rā. Nāku noa, nā (ingoa).
Enough said. Take care. Yours sincerely, (name).

4. Kāore e tōia ngā kōrero kia roa. Noho mai i roto i ngā tūporetanga o te wā. Nā (ingoa).
I've gone on long enough. All the best. From (name).

5. Ā kāti. Hei konā mai i roto i ngā mihi. Nāku noa, nā (ingoa).
Enough said. Many thanks. Yours sincerely (name).

Note that the word *nāku* is for one person only. To sign off for two people, use *'nā māua (noa), nā . . .',* and to sign off for three or more people, use *'nā mātou (noa), nā . . .'.*

KUPU WHAI TAKE
HANDY WORDS

A good way of increasing your usage of te reo Māori, the growth of your te reo knowledge and the normalisation of te reo is to not just have the 'reo sandwich', with Māori at the start and end of your communications (with English 'sandwiched' in the middle), but to 'sprinkle' Māori terms and phrases throughout, whether it be a text, an email, a social media post or any one of the many forms of communication styles the modern world entails.

Below are some words and phrases to help you.

Mahi – work/task/job
But that's enough talk about *mahi*. How have you been anyway?
We need to do more on that *mahi*.

See you at *mahi* next week.

We all have a lot of *mahi* on, but it's important to keep our communication going.

Mahi will finish at 3 p.m. today so we can all go home and celebrate Matariki.

Kōrero – talk/communicate; information

The latest *kōrero* I have to share is this . . .

We will be meeting in the lunchroom at 12 p.m. to have a *kōrero* about the business.

I had a *kōrero* to the boss yesterday – it's not looking good.

Who wants to do the *kōrero* about current sales stats?

It would be good to have a catch-up. Maybe a coffee and a *kōrero* before work?

Hui – gather/meet; meeting

The all-staff *hui* will now be at 3 p.m.

We are having a breakfast *hui* tomorrow – you should come.

Go and have a *hui* with Tania. She will know what to do.

We have had a lot of *hui* about this, so hopefully we can move forward.

I had a really good *hui* with Meihana yesterday.

Kai – food/meal

It would be great if everyone brought some *kai*.

There will be *kai* available for purchase.

Go to this restaurant – the *kai* is fantastic!

Let's go for a *kai* this afternoon!
I'd just like to thank whoever brought the *kai* to work today
– awesome!

Aroha – sympathy/compassion/love
Sending all my *aroha* to you all at this difficult time.
I think there is a bit of *aroha* growing between those two.
Redundancies are always very difficult, so please show
some *aroha* to your fellow workers.
The values we respect the most include *aroha* and working
together.
Ka aroha – I feel for you.

Auē / Aue – heck/oh dear (to express surprise)
Auē! I'm rambling now, so I better sign off!
Did you hear about Helen? *Auē*!
I'm worried about Cynthia, *aue*.
Who left all the dishes in the sink? *Auē*!
Aue! It's nearly Christmas already!

Koha – gift/present
As we all know, Maire is leaving us, so we are going to get
her a leaving *koha*.
All staff are asked to not touch the *koha* we have in the
staffroom.
I'm going to buy a *koha* for Mum, for Mother's Day. Do you
want to chip in?

There is chocolate cake in the kitchen – it's a *koha* from the board for all our hard work.

There will be a gold-coin *koha* on entry.

Tangi – funeral; to cry

Anyone who wants to attend the *tangi* is most welcome to do so.

The *tangi* will be three days long and will be held in Rotorua.

Redundancies are a difficult time, so please feel free to use our support services to have a *kōrero* and a *tangi* if needed.

We do have *tangi* leave available.

Does anyone know an appropriate song we can sing at her *tangi*?

Tautoko – support

We would like to extend our *tautoko* at this time.

Best wishes and *tautoko* for your new venture.

I need you to come and *tautoko*.

Harry, I think what you said in the meeting was absolutely correct, *tautoko*!

I need everybody to *tautoko* so we can push this at our next board meeting.

Kaupapa – plan/agenda/topic/scheme/proposal

There are quite a few *kaupapa* to cover in this email, so please bear with me.

Are there any more *kaupapa* to add?

The *kaupapa* for this week is the environment.

What's the *kaupapa* of the meeting?

I have a huge *kaupapa* that I would like advice on. Are you free tomorrow?

RERENGA WHAI TAKE
HANDY PHRASES

E pai ana – all good/okay/sweet as

We didn't get to our goal, but *e pai ana*.

Just a note to staff, if you want to leave early today, *e pai ana*.

Do you want to meet at the café later? *E pai ana*?

You made a mistake but, *e pai ana*, it's not the end of the world!

Mere, with regards to your request, *e pai ana*, but only until the end of the week.

Hēoi anō – accordingly/and so/but/however (denotes completeness or sufficiency)

Okay, so we didn't get the result we wanted – *hēoi anō*, I'm still proud of the effort!

Betty will be leaving on Thursday, *hēoi anō*, this doesn't mean we all stop working!

Hēoi anō, that's enough for now. See you next week!

Hēoi anō, this is a good time to refocus our efforts.

He gave me half the house, *hēoi anō*.

Kawea te mānuka – take up the challenge

We need to improve this year. *Kawea te mānuka* . . . let's do this!

Some of you might be unsure of what your new positions entail, but *kawea te mānuka*!

Mate, this is a wonderful opportunity – *kawea te mānuka!*

Our netball team has made the finals this weekend. *Kawea te mānuka* – good luck!

So, I just want to ask: who will *kawea te mānuka* and accept the new proposal?

Māmā noa iho – easy as/no sweat/no worries

This is not a difficult task – its actually *māmā noa iho*.

Māmā noa iho to give up but you will regret it if you do.

Hey boss, just replying to your request – I will do it. *Māmā noa iho!*

I'll go and get the alcohol. *Māmā noa iho!*

We will beat them on Saturday, you watch. *Māmā noa iho!*

Kia tau – settle down/don't panic/chill out/be calm

This is a time when we all just need to *kia tau* and work things out.

Kia tau Henry, you are out of line!

I realise doing the dishes is a big deal to some, but can we just *kia tau* a bit please?

If you are using this space, *kia tau*!

If she blows up again just tell her to *kia tau!*

NGĀ HUI
MEETINGS

Hui is a word that has become normalised in everyday New Zealand language and is used to articulate a gathering or the assembly of people to discuss a particular project, issue or topic. In other words, it's Māori for a meeting – and so, 'Let's have a *hui* about it' = 'Let's have a *meeting* about it.' In traditional times, a hui was called for many reasons and usually held on the marae, the central and focal point of the village. In fact, if anything big was happening, a hui would always be held at the marae, and to this day it's still the same! How cool is that? Weddings, birthdays, funerals, graduations, political debates, environmental discussions . . . you name it, it's held at the marae.

Now, protocols or *tikanga* were followed to ensure any discussions held during a hui were respectful and conciliatory, and many businesses and organisations today use these protocols to conduct their hui with those objectives in mind. They are another example of the value that Māori principles and tikanga can provide in modern settings (read more on this in the Tikanga chapter on page 180). So, let's take a look at how we would run our meeting or hui, guided by Māori protocols or tikanga:

Karakia – we start the hui with a *karakia*. Karakia can be contentious and confronting to some because of the misconception that all karakia have a religious origin, theme or purpose. They have become a flashpoint for racism and division in many workplaces and communities, such as local councils. However, there are many different karakia for every type of occasion. Some talk about and refer to traditional Māori deities, some have a Christian base. The type of karakia I usually select to begin a hui with multiple personalities and ethnicities present is one that fuses and enhances energy, and encourages a high-level focus on the issue in front of the group attending the meeting. This is the value of beginning with a karakia – it is a call to attention, a call to unite, a call to be present and ready, and a call to focus. (For more on karakia, see page 185.)

Here is an example of a good karakia to begin with:

Tūtawa mai i runga.	*I summon from above.*
Tūtawa mai i raro.	*I summon from below.*
Tūtawa mai i roto.	*I summon from within.*
Tūtawa mai i roto.	*I summon from the environment that surrounds us.*

Kia tau ai te mauri tū	*Vitality, energy, and well-being*
te mauri ora ki te katoa.	*to sustain all who are present.*
Hāumi e, hui e, tāiki e!	*To unite in common purpose!*

(Note: everybody present says the *tāiki e!* together.)

Mihimihi – this tikanga is based on the principle of *whanaungatanga*. It is a chance to acknowledge who everybody is and where they come from. Building whanaungatanga is vital to the success of any team, business or project because it emphasises the 'we' and not the 'me'. Whanaungatanga builds kinship ties and places value on who each person is, recognising all the knowledge, understandings and experiences they bring to enhance the collective. It can be as simple as going around the room and giving people an opportunity to say who they are and where they come from before you get into the business of the hui. The coordinator of the hui might like to start with a basic mihi, followed by introducing him- or herself as follows:

Kei te mihi ki te rangi.	*I pay acknowledgement to the sky above.*
Kei te mihi ki te whenua.	*I pay acknowledgement to the earth below.*

Kei te mihi ki te kaikarakia.	*I pay acknowledgement to the person who led the blessing.*
Kei te mihi ki ngā mate, haere atu rā.	*I pay acknowledgement to those who have passed.*
(Short pause here)	
Kei te mihi ki a tatou e hui nei.	*I pay acknowledgement to all of us here.*
Tēnā koutou, tēna koutou, nau mai!	*Greetings and welcome.*
Ko . . . ahau.	*My name is . . .*
Nō . . . ahau.	*I am from . . .*
Kia ora koutou!	*Greetings once again!*

Pepeha – a traditional Māori way to introduce yourself is by using *pepeha*. This is done by reciting the mountains, land and water that connect us to our ancestors, to our tribal areas and to our natural surroundings. Pepeha encourages us to go on a journey of discovery to find out who we are, who our ancestors are and where we originate from. It can be difficult, emotional and confronting for many, including Māori who were disconnected from their culture by colonisation.

For Māori, pepeha are the equivalent of a tribal motto, in which we reference landmarks and ancestors we connect to through whakapapa. It is an inherited connection to a place, regardless of whether you were raised there or not.

You are also introducing yourself as part of the collective – that is, as part of your tribe – and with that comes the responsibility of being a member of that tribal group.

For example, I would say, 'Ko Ngāti Whakaue tōku / te iwi' – 'I am part of the Whakaue tribal confederation,' or, 'I am one of the descendants of the ancestor, Whakaue.'

For non-Māori, a pepeha is usually based on lived experience in a particular place that becomes close to their heart and, therefore, becomes their 'home base'. In many cases, the traditional pepeha format of maunga (mountain), awa/moana (waterway), iwi (tribe), hapū (subtribe) and marae (home base) will not be appropriate, unless reciting your heritage connection – for example, the landmarks that identify the ancestry and origin of your Irish whakapapa or Indian whakapapa.

However, you might still have a strong lived connection with places in Aotearoa, so, as a non-Māori, your pepeha could look something like this:

1. Firstly, acknowledge and establish where your ancestors are from (i.e. your whakapapa), for example:

Nō Inia ōku tūpuna.

My ancestors are from India.

2. Now you can acknowledge the mountain you connect with in Aotearoa or where you are currently living by saying something like:

I tipu ake au i ngā rekereke o te maunga o . . .

I grew up at the foot of . . . mountain.

Kei te maru o te maunga o . . . ahau e noho ana.
I live under the protection of . . . mountain.

3. Then you can acknowledge the awa or moana by saying:
Ko . . . te moana/awa.
The waterway is . . .

4. And then acknowledge the local tribe but be sure to research this properly – sometimes, there are many tribes in one particular area. Their boundaries will be identifiable:
Ko . . . te mana whenua.
. . . are the local tribe.

5. And finally, your name:
Ko . . . ahau.
I am . . .

Always finish off with:
Tēnā koutou, tēnā koutou, tēnā koutou!

Hongi – you may want to conclude the mihimihi part of the hui with the *hongi* or the gentle pressing of noses. The hongi is a tradition that stems from our ancient narratives about the creation of people and the pressing of the nose of Tāne onto Hineahuone's, to transmit the *mauri* or life force to her and, in so doing, bring to life the first human being. It is a very sacred, very personal exchange but can enhance other Māori principles utilised in the workplace like *kotahitanga* or unity and *manaakitanga* or the respect and care of a person's integrity or *mana*. Now, everybody has a funny hongi story so don't get too upset or embarrassed of it doesn't go well; it takes a bit of practice to do a good hongi and be comfortable with it. (Read more on this in the Hongi and Harirū section on page 192.)

Into the mahi – after the meeting has been opened following tikanga practices of karakia, mihimihi, pepeha (optional) and hongi (optional), it's into the *mahi* or the task at hand! A good tip is to think about the seating arrangements, keeping in mind the 'we' and not 'me' theme. You want to be inclusive, so no 'levels' of seating – for example, some sitting higher than others or sitting in a different style of chair (like a throne or something, yuck!). Try not to have barriers in front of people either, like sitting in behind tables or lecterns. If possible, arrange the seating in a circle, so everybody is *kanohi ki te kanohi*, or face to face, encouraging a sense of togetherness, a sense of community, a sense of whanaungatanga!

Karakia – end the hui with a karakia to bring things to an close, to clear any angst or negativity that has occurred and to restore balance for people to return to their daily routines and everyday lives. Here is a simple karakia to use for this purpose:

Tahia te tahua.	*I clear away any obstructions.*
Tahia te tahua.	*I clear away any negativity.*

Turuki whakataha.   *I push them to the side.*
Turuki whakataha.   *I push them away.*
Haumi e, hui e, tāiki e!   *We leave in positivity and*
                              in unity, 'tis done!

RERENGA WHAI TAKE
HANDY PHRASES

Let's start with some greetings – the first words you use
when you arrive at a hui:

Kia ora.
Hello.

Kei te pēhea koe?
How are you?

Kei te pai.
Good.

A koe?
And you?

Kei te harikoa au.
I am happy.

Kei te ngenge au.
I am tired.

Kei te maremare au.
I have a bit of a cold.

Ka kite anō.
See you later.

Hei te wā.
Catch you up.

Ngā manaakitanga.
All the best.

Now that you've 'broken the ice' with other attendees of the hui, here are a few conversation starters:

Kua rongo koe mō . . . (ingoa o te tangata)?
Have you heard about . . . (name of person)?

Kua tauwehe rāua.
They (2) have split up.

I mau ia.
He/She/They (singular) got caught.

Kāti te whawhewhawhe.
Stop gossiping.

Hika mā, he kino te huarere i te rā nei!
Gosh, the weather is terrible today!

Hika mā, i kino te huarahi i te rā nei!
Wow, the traffic was shocking this morning!

Hika mā, kei te tino piki te utu mō te kai!
Gosh, food prices are skyrocketing!

Hika mā, he kino te muia o ngā huarahi i Tāmaki!
Wow, Auckland has a terrible traffic problem!

Hurō! Kua tae mai te Rāmere!
Hooray! Thank God it's Friday!

I aha koe i ngā rangi whakatā nei?
What did you (1 person) get up to over the weekend?

Kei te aha koe a ēnei rangi whakatā?
What are you (1 person) up to this weekend?

E hika, kua toru karaka kē!
Wow, I can't believe it's 3 p.m. already!

E hika, kua tōroa marika tēnei hui.
Wow, this meeting has dragged on forever.

Auē, kei te tino rongo au i te whiu a te waipiro.
Gosh, I am terribly hungover.

Kei te huitopa au i te kāinga i te rā nei.
I'm joining via Zoom from home today.

Kei te huitopa au i te kāinga āpōpō.
I'm joining via Zoom from home tomorrow.

Kei te huitopa au i te kāinga a tērā wiki.
I'm joining via Zoom from home next week.

WHAIKŌRERO
SPEECHES

In this section of the book, you get the chance to build your own speech to use during formal occasions. Most Māori speakers will follow a general format but this can vary, and the type and length of language used will depend on the ability of the speaker.

You will notice the language of whaikōrero is much more metaphorical than everyday language. It's a very eloquent style of language that sometimes may seem a bit weird in English, but just go with it, e hoa mā!

It takes a lifetime to perfect the art and become a lead speaker for your tribe, so the main thing for you to remember at this stage is that if you get asked to speak on behalf of a group, your workplace or at a formal event, be humble, practise and deliver the appropriate mihi or acknowledgements to the right people and places.

Here are some sample whaikōrero for you to learn. As I mentioned before, it will generally follow a set pattern:

1. Begin with a *tauparapara* or evocation, to grab the audience's attention.
2. The second stage is to acknowledge the building you are in and the land you are standing on. This is called *mihi whare* and *mihi whenua*.
3. The next part is to pay tribute to those who have passed on – this is called *mihi mate*.
4. After the *mihi mate* has been completed, you can then focus on the topic or issue of the day that has brought you all together – *mihi i te kaupapa* – acknowledge the theme of the day.
5. Conclusion or *whakatepe*.

After the *whakatepe* or final remarks, it is expected that you perform a waiata or song to conclude your speech in the appropriate way. This is called a *whakarehu* and symbolically releases you from the transcendental position you were just in. *Kia māngari*! Good luck!

BUILD YOUR WHAIKŌRERO

Take <u>one</u> line from each of the five sections (each section has five lines or options to choose from) and create a whaikōrero.

Each section starts with some basic lines that are nice and short. The lines will then get more and more technical, more and more poetical and metaphorical . . . and much longer! You need to ascertain what you can handle, what your level of capability is, and how much time you have to learn the speech (with correct pronunciation). You will end up with one line from each of parts one to five . . . and *mea rawa ake* or *voilà*! You have a speech!

PART ONE – CHOOSE A WHAKAOHOOHO

1. Tihei mauri ora!
I exhort the breath of life!

2. E ngā rangatira, tēnā koutou, tēnā koutou, tēnā koutou katoa.
To my esteemed colleagues/guests, I greet you all.

3. E ngā hau e whā, tēnā koutou, tēnā koutou, tēnā koutou katoa.
To those from the four winds, I greet you all.

4. E ngā tai e whā o te motu, tēnā koutou, tēnā koutou, tēnā koutou katoa.
To those from all four directions across the country, I greet you all.

5. E ngā rau o te kōtuku e huihui mai nei, tēnā koutou, tēnā koutou, tēnā koutou katoa.
To the plumes of the white heron gathered here today, I greet you all.

Other appropriate proverbs you could start with (along with the phrase 'E kī ana te kōrero' preceding them), include:

Ehara taku toa i te toa takitahi, engari he toa takitini.
My strength is not mine alone, it comes from the collective/ from the group.

E haunui ana i raro, e hari ana i runga.
It's blustery below but the sky above is clear (The difficult times are over, the way ahead is now easier).

Kei whawhati noa mai te rau o te rātā.
Don't pluck the blossoms of the rātā tree (Some things are perfect just the way they are).

E ngaki ana ā mua, e tōtō mai ana a muri.
If the first group do the work properly, the following group can accomplish the task.

He iti hau marangai e tū te pāhokahoka.
Just like a rainbow after the storm, success follows failure.

PART TWO – CHOOSE A MIHI WHARE/ MIHI WHENUA

1. E te whare, e te papa, tēnā kōrua.
This house, this land, I greet you both.

2. E te whare whakaruruhau, e te whenua waiū tāngata, tēnā kōrua.

The sheltering building, the nurturing land, I greet you both.

3. Te whare e tū nei, te marae e hora nei, te iwi e tau nei, tēnā koutou katoa.
The house that stands before me, the sacred ground that stretches below me, and all the people gathered here today, I greet you all.

4. E te whare ātaahua e tū nei, tēnā koe. E te whenua taurikura e takoto nei, tēnā koe.
I greet this beautiful house standing here. I greet this precious land lying here.

5. Tāne whakapiripiri e tū nei; Rongomaraeroa e takoto nei – tēnā kōrua.
The house of the god of the forest, Tāne; the land of the god of peace, Rongo – I greet you both.

Note that the words *whare* or *whenua* are considered to be symbols of the Māori world that remind us of our ancestors and our history. Other symbols contained in these types of mihi might be mountains, rivers, lakes, spiritual beings and any other symbols of the old world still present with us today.

PART THREE – CHOOSE A MIHI MATE

1. E ngā mate, haere atu rā.
To those who have passed, I farewell you all.

2. E ngā aituā maha, haere atu rā.
To the many who have passed, I farewell you all.

3. E ngā pare raukura o te mate, haere, haere, haere atu rā.
To the exalted ones no longer with us, I farewell you all.

4. Ki ngā raukura kua maunu atu ki moana uriuri, haere, haere, haere atu rā.
To the exalted who have drifted off to the depths of the great ocean, I farewell you all.

5. Ki ngā huia kaimanawa kua ngaro ki te pō, moe mai koutou.
To our precious ones who have disappeared into the night, rest in peace.

Note that when you finish the *mihi mate*, make sure you utter this statement to show separation between your words to the deceased and your words to the living:

Rātou ki a rātou
Tātou ki a tātou

PART FOUR – CHOOSE A MIHI I TE KAUPAPA

1. E mihi ana ki te kaupapa o te rā.
I acknowledge the reason for today's gathering.

2. E mihi ana ki te kaupapa e whakahuihui nei i a tātou.
I acknowledge the topical issue that has gathered us together today.

3. He rā whakahirahira tēnei mō tātou katoa, he kaupapa nui kei mua i a tātou.
This is indeed a special day for us all, an important occasion lies before us.

4. E mihi ana ki a tātou i te whakaaro nui kia tae mai tātou ki tēnei kaupapa i te rā nei.
I acknowledge all of us who have prioritised being here today for this important occasion.

5. Ka mihi te ngākau ki a koutou kua tae mai, i te tī, i te tā, ki te tautoko i te kaupapa o te rā.
My heartfelt thank you to all of you who have come from many different places to support this occasion today.

PART FIVE – CHOOSE A MIHI WHAKATEPE

1. Nō reira, tēnā koutou, tēnā koutou, tēnā koutou katoa.
And so I greet you all once again, thank you.

2. Nō reira, kāti i konei. Tēnā koutou, tēnā koutou, tēnā koutou katoa.
And so let me conclude at this point. I greet you all once again, thank you.

3. Nō reira, kāti i konei. Ngā manaakitanga o te wā ki a koutou katoa. Tēnā koutou, tēnā koutou, tēnā koutou katoa.
And so let me conclude at this point. I wish you all the best. I greet you all once again, thank you.

4. Ahakoa he mihi poto tēnei, he mihi aroha. Nō reira e hoa mā, tēnā koutou, tēnā koutou, tēnā koutou katoa.
Although this greeting is short, it is from the heart with love. Therefore, my friends, greetings to us all.

5. Nō reira e mihi ana ki a koutou i roto i ngā manaakitanga o te rā nei, tēnā koutou, tēnā koutou, tēnā tātou katoa.
And so I offer greetings again and hope today brings good tidings to all, thank you very much.

If you sit down for a meal at an important occasion, it is customary for visitors to make a short speech towards the end or at the conclusion of the hākari. Here is an example for you to learn; and don't forget your *whakarehu* or song.

Tihei mauri ora!
I exhort the breath of life!

E ngā tohunga o te manaaki tangata.
My supreme hosts.

Me pehea rā e rite ai i a au tā koutou whakautetanga mai i tēnei rā?
How can I ever repay your hospitality on this day?

Ka hau te rongo mō koutou, nō reira tēnā koutou!
It will be spoken about in times to come, and so I thank you very much!

Te reka o te kai!
The delicious meal!

Te pai o te tangata!
The wonderful people!

Tē hiahia hoki atu!
One does not wish to leave!

Noho ake me te aroha.
Farewell, we leave you with our affection.

Kia ora tātou katoa!
Greetings again to us all!

NGĀ NAMA ME TE WĀ
NUMBERS AND TIME

NAMA
NUMBERS

Knowing numbers in any language is critical, especially when keeping scores in games against the kids! But apart from that, numbers of course help us to collect information, to organise dates and times for meetings, to analyse data, and so much more.

The Māori number system is an interesting one because it articulates each place value. For example, in English you would simply say eleven for the number 11; in te reo Māori, you would say 'ten plus one' – tekau (10) mā tahi (1). So:

To say the number **25**, you would say the equivalent of two tens and five – rua tekau mā rima.

To say the number **63**, you would say the equivalent of six tens and three – ono tekau mā toru.

To say the number **99**, you would say the equivalent of nine tens and nine – iwa tekau mā iwa.

To say the number **138**, you would say the equivalent of one hundred, three tens and eight – kotahi rau, toru tekau mā waru.

To say the number **546**, you would say the equivalent of five hundreds, four tens and six – e rima rau, whā tekau mā ono.

Cardinal numbers used for counting are as follows:

Tahi	*One*
Rua	*Two*
Toru	*Three*
Whā	*Four*
Rima	*Five*
Ono	*Six*
Whitu	*Seven*
Waru	*Eight*
Iwa	*Nine*
Tekau	*Ten*
Tekau mā tahi	*Eleven*
Tekau mā rua	*Twelve*
Tekau mā toru	*Thirteen*
Tekau mā whā	*Fourteen*
Tekau mā rima	*Fifteen*

Tekau mā ono	*Sixteen*
Tekau mā whitu	*Seventeen*
Tekau mā waru	*Eighteen*
Tekau mā iwa	*Nineteen*
Rua tekau	*Twenty*
Rua tekau mā tahi	*Twenty-one*
Toru tekau	*Thirty*
Whā tekau	*Forty*
Rima tekau	*Fifty*
Ono tekau	*Sixty*
Whitu tekau	*Seventy*
Waru tekau	*Eighty*
Iwa tekau	*Ninety*
Kotahi rau	*One hundred*
Rua rau	*Two hundred*
Kotahi mano	*One thousand*
Kotahi miriona	*One million*

Ordinal numbers used for ranking between one and nine require the prefix *tua*:

Tuatahi	*First*
Tuarua	*Second*
Tuatoru	*Third*

I tuawhā ia.
He/She/They (singular) came fourth.

Wāhanga tuarima.
Chapter five.

Kei te papa tuaono tōna whare.
His/Her/Their (singular) apartment is on the sixth floor.

Ordinal numbers from 10 upwards require no prefix:

Tekau mā rima	*Fifteenth*
Waru tekau mā ono	*Eighty-sixth*

This is the format for years:

Rua mano mā tahi	*2001*
Rua mano tekau mā tahi	*2011*
Kotahi mano, iwa rau,	
waru tekau mā waru	*1988*

When asking about how many items or objects there are, use *e hia*:

E hia ngā āporo?
How many apples are there?

E whitu ngā āporo.
There are seven apples.

E hia ōku matimati?
How many fingers do I have?

E rima ō matimati.
You have five fingers.

E hia ngā hōiho o tēnei tauwhāinga?
How many horses are in this race?

Tekau ma whā.
Fourteen.

When asking how many people there are, use the prefix *toko*. When responding, use *toko* only when the number of people being spoken about is between two and nine:

Tokohia ngā tāngata kei te haere mai?
How many people are coming?

Tokowaru.
Eight.

Tokohia ō tamariki?
How many children do you have?

Tokotoru aku tamariki.
I have three children.

Tokohia ngā wāhine o tēnei kapa?
How many women in this team?

Tekau mā rua.
Twelve.

Tokohia ngā tāngata i haere?
How many people went?

Kotahi rau, ono tekau mā whā.
164.

When asking how many items or objects are required, use *kia hia*:

Kia hia ngā pukapuka māu?
How many books do you want?

Kia whitu ngā pukapuka māku.
Seven books for me.

Kia hia ngā inu mā koutou?
How many drinks do you (three or more) want?

Kia rua tekau mā whā ngā inu.
Two dozen (24).

Homai kia kotahi te tōtiti, kia rua ngā hēki.
(Can I have) one sausage and two eggs.

Kia kotahi anō ka mutu.
One more then finish.

When indicating there is only one, *kotahi* is used, irrespective of whether it indicates people or objects:

Kotahi te rangatira.
There is only one leader.

Kotahi te whakautu.
There is only one answer.

Kotahi te māngai mō tātou.
There is only one spokesperson for us.

Kotahi te rongoā.
There is only one remedy.

E hia te utu? and sometimes *He aha te utu?* are acceptable ways of asking for the cost or price of an item. The words *tāra* for dollars and *hēneti* for cents are commonly used in the response.

E hia te utu mō/o tēnei waka?
How much does this car cost?

Tekau mano tāra te utu mō/o tēnei waka.
This car costs 10,000 dollars.

E hia te utu mō/o te parāoa?
How much for the bread?

E rua tāra.
Two dollars.

Anei ō inu, e tā.
Here are your drinks, sir.

Tēnā koe, e hia te utu?
Thank you, how much do I owe you?

E whitu tāra, e waru tekau hēneti.
Seven dollars and eighty cents.

TE WĀ
TIME

He aha te wā? and *Ko te aha te wā?* are two common ways of asking what the time is. Language experts also recommend *Kua aha te wā?* which is what I use the most. *Karaka* is the equivalent of 'o'clock', *hāora* is 'hours', *meneti* is 'minutes'. Māori follow three general daily time zones, *ata* from midnight to midday, *ahiahi* from midday to dusk, and *pō* from dusk to midnight.

Kua aha te wā?	*What's the time?*
Kua whitu karaka	*Seven o'clock*
Kua tekau karaka i te ata	*10 a.m.*
Kua toru karaka i te ahiahi	*3 p.m.*
Kua waru karaka i te pō	*8 p.m.*
Kua tekau meneti i te ono	*Ten past six*
Kua rua tekau mā whā meneti i te iwa i te pō	*9:24 p.m.*

It is important to know the following terms:

Hauwhā ki . . .	*Quarter to . . .*
Hauwhā i . . .	*Quarter past . . .*
Haurua i . . .	*Half past . . .*
Waenganui pō	*Midnight*
Poupoutanga o te rā	*Midday*
Atatū	*Dawn*

So you are able to say:

Me hui tātou ā te hauwhā ki te tekau.
Let's meet at quarter to 10.

Hauwhā i te iwa karaka i te ata te wā.
It's 9:15 a.m.

He aha te wā tae mai o ngā tamariki? / Āhea ngā tamariki
tae mai ai?
What time do the children arrive?

Haurua i te rua ā te ahiahi.
2:30 p.m.

He aha te wā mutu o te ngahau nei? / Āhea te ngahau nei
mutu ai?
What time does this party finish?

Waenganui pō.
Midnight.

Words that start with '*i*' usually indicate past tense:

Inahea?	*When?*
Inanahi	*Yesterday*
Inatahirā	*The day before yesterday*
I tērā wiki	*Last week*
I tērā marama	*Last month*
I tērā tau	*Last year*
I tērā Rāpare	*Last Thursday*

I haere au ki tō Mere inapō.
I went to Mere's house last night.

I hoko kai au māu.
I bought you some food.

I tae mai te kōrero inanahi.
The news came yesterday.

I taua wā e ranea ana te kai.
At that time there was plenty of food.

The following words indicate present-tense actions and
time:

Ināianei	*Now*
I tēnei wā	*At this time*
I tēnei rā	*Today*

Kei te haere au ināianei.
I am leaving now.

E tākaro ana rātou i tēnei wā.
They (three or more) are playing now.

Ka pakanga ngā kapa i tēnei rā.
The teams will do battle today.

Words and phrases that begin with '*ā*' usually indicate future time or tense:

Āhea?	*When?*
Āpōpō	*Tomorrow*
Ātahirā	*The day after tomorrow*
Ā tērā wiki	*Next week*
Ā tērā marama	*Next month*
Ā tērā tau	*Next year*
Ā tērā Rāapa	*Next Wednesday*
Ā te wā	*In due course*

Ka haere māua ki tō Hēmi ā te pō nei.
We (us two) will go to Hēmi's house tonight.

Waiho mō āpōpō.
Leave it for tomorrow.

Ka tae mai ngā manuhiri ā tērā wiki.
The visitors arrive next week.

Ā te wā, ka kite koe i te hua o āu mahi.
In due course, you will see the fruits of your labour.

Other important phrases to know:

Kua awatea.
It is daylight/daybreak.

Kua pō.
It is night-time.

Kua tō te rā.
The sun has set.

Kei te whiti te rā.
The sun is shining.

Kei te tiaho te marama.
The moon is gleaming.

Kei te kōrikoriko ngā whetū.
The stars are sparkling.

Ā te ata āpōpō.
Tomorrow morning.

Hei te atatū.
Early in the morning.

Hei te ahiahi āpōpō.
Tomorrow afternoon.

Moata rawa.
It's too early.

Tōmuri rawa.
It's too late.

Āhea te haerenga ka tīmata?
When does the tour begin?

Kei te tōmuri tātou!
We (three or more) are late!

Auē, kia tere!
Oh no, hurry up!

Taihoa!
Hang on a minute!

Me haere tātou!
Let's (three or more) go!

Ia rā.
Every day.

Ia hāora.
Every hour.

Ia haurua hāora, ka wehe te pahi.
The bus departs every half hour.

Ia tekau mā rima meneti, ka rato he kai.
Food is served every 15 minutes.

NGĀ RĀ, NGĀ MARAMA ME NGĀ TAU
DAYS, MONTHS AND YEARS

In our everyday lives, we follow what's called the Gregorian calendar, which is a solar calendar, so it is advised to use the 'loan' Māori words like *Hānuere* for January and *Pēpuere* for February when speaking about the months of the year, and *Mane* for Monday and *Tūrei* for Tuesday when speaking about the days of the week.

All months of the maramataka Māori or the Māori lunar calendar get their names from the star that rises before the sun at a particular time of the year. Naturally, the star passes and is replaced by a new one every 28 days, which indicates a new month. So, applying the traditional Māori names for the months of the year to the Gregorian calendar doesn't really work, as it becomes out of sync, because we are applying lunar phases to the phases and movements of the sun. In addition to this, there are only 354 days in the maramataka Māori, 11 days fewer than the Gregorian calendar. The maramataka Māori is reset every three years, with a 33-day month called *Ruhanui*.

NGĀ RĀ
DAYS

Rāhina (*Monday*)	or: Mane
Rātū (*Tuesday*)	or: Tūrei
Rāapa (*Wednesday*)	or: Wenerei
Rāpare (*Thursday*)	or: Tāite
Rāmere (*Friday*)	or: Paraire
Rāhoroi (*Saturday*)	
Rātapu (*Sunday*)	

The days of the week on the left are based on Māori lunar phases and celestial knowledge of our ancestors. The ones on the right are *kupu arotau* or borrowed words from English (otherwise known as transliterations or 'loan' words). *Rā* is the word for day, so:

Rāhina acknowledges the importance of the moon and uses a shortened version of an ancient name for the moon, *Māhina*. The more common name for the moon that you may hear in everyday conversations is *marama*.

Me tūtaki tāua ā te Rāhina/Mane.
Let's (you and I) meet on Monday.

Rātū acknowledges the planet Mars or *Tūmatauenga*. Another name for Mars is Matawhero. Tūmatauenga is also the Māori god of war, and like many other indigenous cultures around the world, its red appearance was sometimes interpreted as a representation of anger and conflict.

Ka tū te hui ā te Rātū/Tūrei.
The meeting will be held on Tuesday.

Rāapa acknowledges the planet Mercury or *Apārangi*. One explanation for this name is that it connects to Hine-te-Apārangi, the wife of Kupe, who was an early explorer and, in some tribal histories, the first to navigate to and around Aotearoa New Zealand. Kupe's wife Hine-te-Apārangi, or Kuramarotini according to some, was with him and was the first to sight the cloud formations above this land, exclaiming from their voyaging waka, 'He ao, he ao, he ao-tea-roa!' This translates to, 'A cloud, a cloud, a long-white-cloud!' Sometimes the planet is called Whiro, which leads us to a totally different version of what this planet represents: Whiro is a deity of darkness and destruction.

Kāore ia i tae mai ki te mahi i te Rāapa/Wenerei.
He/She/They (singular) didn't come to work on Wednesday.

Rāpare honours another female planet, Jupiter or *Pareārau*. At times, Pareārau ('Pare of a hundred lovers') sits very close to the planet Venus in the night sky. However, there are other nights where it appears Pareārau has 'wandered away' from her husband, Venus, to see what else is out there! The planet Jupiter is also known as Hinetīweka in some tribal areas, or 'wayward Hine'. Another name for Jupiter is Kōpūnui, because of its size. Pareārau is the name for Saturn in many tribal areas.

Ia Rāpare/Tāite, hoko tina ai tō mātou tumuaki mā mātou.
Our boss buys us lunch every Thursday.

Rāmere is named after the poor husband of Pareārau, Venus or *Meremere*. Venus has many other names, too. It can be Tāwera when viewed in the early morning, and in this form as the morning 'star', this planet is male! Then, when seen in the light of the late afternoon, it becomes female, known as Meremere or Meremere-tū-ahiahi, revered for her exquisite beauty! At times of the year this planet is also known as Kōpū; a good time for people to get 'closer', if you know what I mean!

Nau mai te Rāmere/Paraire!
Welcome Friday! (i.e. 'Thank God it's Friday!')

RERENGA WHAI TAKE
HANDY PHRASES

Ko te aha tēnei rā?
What day is it?

Rātū.
Tuesday.

Ko te Rāhina tēnei rā.
Today is Monday.

Ko te aha tēnei rā?
What is the day/date today?

Ko te Tūrei.
Tuesday.

Ka kōrero ia ki te tumu whakahaere ā te Rāmere.
He/She will talk to the manager on Friday.

Āhea koe haere ai?
When do you leave?

Ā te Rātapu.
On Sunday.

Āhea koe hoki mai ai?
When do you return?

Aua, ā te Rāhoroi pea.
I don't know, maybe Saturday.

Ka tae mai ngā manuhiri nō Haina ā te Rāapa.
The Chinese guests arrive on Wednesday.

Kāore au i te mahi ā te Rāhina.
I won't be at work on Monday.

I tamō ia i te Rāpare.
He/She was absent on Thursday.

I whara au i te Rāhina i te wāhi mahi.
I got injured on Monday at work.

NGĀ MARAMA
MONTHS

Kohitātea (*January*)	or: Hānuere
Huitanguru (*February*)	or: Pēpuere
Poutūterangi (*March*)	or: Māehe
Paengawhāwhā (*April*)	or: Āperira
Haratua (*May*)	or: Mei
Pipiri (*June*)	or: Hune
Hōngongoi (*July*)	or: Hūrae
Hereturikōkā (*August*)	or: Ākuhata
Mahuru (*September*)	or: Hepetema
Whiringa-ā-nuku (*October*)	or: Oketopa
Whiringa-ā-rangi (*November*)	or: Noema
Hakihea (*December*)	or: Tīhema

Don't forget, the words for the months of the year on the left are based on Māori perceptions of the environment, names of stars and the knowledge of our ancestors regarding seasonal change during the year. Their timeframes are based on the lunar calendar or the phases of the moon, so will differ from the Gregorian calendar we now use. As with the days of the week, the months on the right are *kupu arotau* or borrowed words from English. Let's have a brief look at what the names on the left represent, beginning with June, the approximate time Matariki or the Māori new year commences.

Pipiri – June

This basically translates as 'to be close' or 'to come close together'. This is the colder time of the year and in order to create heat we need to be close and to huddle together.

Ka pau te wā tuku tono ā te marama o Pipiri.
Applications close in June.

Hōngongoi – July

The cold has now become hard to bear and fires need to be lit to ensure survival against the elements. *Hōngongoi* literally means to 'crouch in front of a fire'.

Ka tīmata tō mahi ki a mātou ā te Hōngongoi.
You start work with us in July.

Hereturikōkā – August

The frequency of sitting close to the heat of the fire during the cold weather has scorched the knees. The position this describes is when you wrap your arms around your knees to draw your legs in to your body to create warmth.

Kei te wehe au i te mahi ā te Hereturikōkā.
I will be leaving my job in August.

Mahuru – September

This denotes the warming of the climate. The earth, the flora and fauna, and even the atmosphere are starting to emerge from the cold of winter to the warmer time of spring. Mahuru is the name for the goddess of spring.

Me tīmata te hanga huarahi hōu ā te Mahuru.
The building of new roads should start in September.

Whiringa-ā-nuku – October

Another word that describes the earth starting to get warmer. The *nuku* part of the word refers to Papatūānuku, the earth mother.

Me tū te whakawhanaunga kaimahi ā te Whiringa-ā-nuku.
We should have the team building in October.

Whiringa-ā-rangi – November

Just as the earth starts to warm, so does the sky, denoting the impending arrival of summer. The sky is becoming increasingly clear and blue. The *rangi* part of the word refers to Ranginui, the sky father.

Ko Whiringa-ā-rangi te marama pai kia timata ki te whakatū whare.
November is the best month to begin to build houses.

Hakihea – December

Birds are in their nests, flowers are abundant and the native pōhutukawa are blooming. All signs of the warm time of summer.

He wā whakatā i te mahi, te Hakihea.
December is the time we take a break from work.

Kohitātea – January

This word literally means to gather the fruits of summer that are now on offer.

E pai ana kia hararei au ā te Kohitātea?
Can I take my holidays in January?

Huitanguru – February

A *tanguru* is a large green beetle that was plentiful around this time, and yes, the ancient Māori used to eat them. (They tasted quite nice, apparently – like a Pineapple Lump. Just kidding!)

Ā te Huitanguru te rauna utu e whai ake nei.
The next pay round is in February.

Poutūterangi – March

This is the name of an important star that rises at this time of the year. It indicated a time to harvest certain crops, such as the kūmara. In the South Island, Te Wai Pounamu, it was also a sign to harvest the famous tītī or muttonbird. Its English name is Altair.

Kei te hoko taraka mahi hōu mō koutou ā te Poutūterangi.
We are buying new work trucks for you (all) in March.

Paengawhāwhā – April

Another word depicting the appropriate time to harvest crops such as kūmara and taro. The word Paengawhāwhā can literally be interpreted as something 'presenting itself for collection by hand'.

Ka mana te poari hōu ā te Paengawhāwhā.
The new board comes into effect in April.

Haratua – May

Final crops are to be collected and stored in preparation for the lean months of winter.

Ko Hēmi te tumu whakahaere tae atu ki te marama o Haratua.
Hēmi is in charge until May.

RERENGA WHAI TAKE
HANDY PHRASES

Ko te tekau mā iwa o Whiringa-ā-rangi taku rā whānau.
My birthday is on the 19th of November.

Āhea tō rā whānau?
When is your birthday?

Ā te tuawhitu o Mahuru.
On the 7th of September.

Ko Poutūterangi te marama tuarua o te tau.
March is the third month of the year.

Hei te marama o Pipiri te tau hou Māori.
The Māori new year is in June.

Ka tū te whakataetae ā te marama o Haratua.
The competition is to be held in May.

Hei te Hakihea te rā Kirihimete.
Christmas is in December.

Hei te kotahi o Kohitātea tō māua mārena.
Our wedding is on the first of January.

I waitohua te Tiriti o Waitangi i te tuaono o Pēpuere.
The Treaty of Waitangi was signed on the 6th of February.

Remember these words come from the traditional Māori lunar or stellar calendar, called the maramataka. The months synchronise with the moon phases, so you may be saying Pipiri for June to line up with the calendar we now follow, but according to the maramataka Māori June or Pipiri may not yet have arrived.

NGĀ TAU
YEARS

The Māori word for year is *tau*. When talking about what *tau* it is, we continue to follow the basic pattern of articulating each place value within the number – that is, thousands, then hundreds, then tens, then ones. Let's take a look:

Thousands / Mano	Hundreds / Rau	Tens / Tekau	Ones / Tahi
1	900	80	3

The above is the year 1983. So, to say this year in Māori, we articulate each number of each column thus – Kotahi mano, e iwa rau, e waru tekau mā toru. The *mā* is very important to connect the tens and the ones columns together. A few more examples for you:

1952 – Kotahi mano, e iwa rau, e rima tekau mā rua
1995 – Kotahi mano, e iwa rau, e iwa tekau mā rima
1840 – Kotahi mano, e waru rau, e whā tekau (note that there is no 'ones' place value)

As you can see, the thousand place value number will remain consistent. In the immediate future, there is only one other number we will use in that column, and that is *rua* or two. We are also a little while away from a number in the hundreds column!

2022 – E rua mano, e rua tekau mā rua (note that there is no 'hundreds' place value)
2010 – E rua mano, tekau
2008 – E rua mano mā waru

And just in case, let's look into the future:

2123 – E rua mano, kotahi rau, e rua tekau mā toru
2225 – E rua mano, e rua rau, rua tekau mā rima

NGĀ HUARERE
WEATHER

Talking about the weather is not only a classic go-to conversation starter, but it also tends to affect our everyday activities. How many times in the day do we refer to the weather? 'It's too cold', 'We'll see what the weather's like', 'We can't go if it rains'. The weather is everywhere, it's ubiquitous, it affects everyone, and some say it even impacts on our emotional states.

Māori often used environmental indicators to predict weather and identify seasonal change.

- If the Mangōroa or the Milky Way was curved, bad weather was approaching. If it was straight, good weather was on the way.
- Early flowering of the tī kōuka or cabbage tree was sign of a long, hot summer.
- If the pōhutukawa began flowering from top to bottom, a cold winter-like season was ahead. If it

flowered from the bottom branches up, a warm and pleasant season was expected.

Migratory birds or bird behaviour was another, holistic way of interpreting the weather conditions.

- If you saw the pūkeko heading for higher ground, it meant that a storm and flooding was imminent.
- If the kārearea or falcon was heard screaming on a fine day, it was expected to rain the next day; and if it screamed on a rainy day, the next day would be fine.
- The arrival of the kuaka or godwit indicated the arrival of warmer conditions.

KUPU WHAI TAKE
HANDY WORDS

Huarere	*Weather*
Tohu huarere	*Weather forecast*
Marino	*Calm weather*
Pūhoro	*Bad weather*
Hātai	*Mild weather*
Ua	*Rain*
Ua kōpatapata	*Spitting*
Ua tarahī	*Light drizzle*
Āwhā	*Storm*
Atiru	*Rain cloud*
Marangai	*Heavy rain*

Paki	*Fine weather*
Kapua	*Cloud*
Kōmaru	*Cloudy*
Hau	*Wind*

RERENGA WHAI TAKE
HANDY PHRASES

Kei te pēhea te rangi?
How is the weather (today/now)?

Ka pēhea te rangi?
What will the weather be (tomorrow/future)?

I pēhea te rangi?
How was the weather?

Te wera hoki, nē?
Gee, it's really hot, isn't it?

Āe mārika!
Yes, it's beautiful!

I te raumati ka marino ngā rā.
The weather is calm in summer.

Te āhua nei ka paki.
It looks like it's going to be fine.

Tatari kia mimiti te hau.
Wait until the wind drops.

Titiro ki te hukapapa!
Look at the frost!

I te takurua ka heke te marangai.
It rains heavily during winter.

He marangai kei te haere mai.
There is heavy rain on the way.

Kua awatea.
It is daylight/daybreak.

Kua pō.
It is night-time.

Kua tō te rā.
The sun has set.

Kei te oho te rā.
It is dawn (the sun is waking up).

Kei te tīaho te marama.
The moon is gleaming.

Kei te kōrikoriko ngā whetū.
The stars are sparkling.

Kaua e titiro ki te rā, ka raru ō karu.
Don't look at the sun – it will damage your eyes.

Kaua e haere ki te ngahere, he kino te matapae huarere.
Don't go to the bush – the weather forecast is not good.

Kaua e haere, e pōrukuruku ana te rangi.
Don't go – the weather is turning bad.

Kaua e parahutihuti te haere, he āwhā āhua taikaha tēnei.
Don't go too fast – this is a pretty bad storm.

Kia tere te oma ki te whare, kei tōpunitia e te ua.
Run quickly to the house or we will get drenched.

Kia tau te noho, kino rawa te ua mō te puta.
Might as well sit down and relax – the rain is too bad to go out.

Kia tūpato, kua tau te kōpaka.
Be careful – it's icy.

Kia hakune te haere, he mōrearea tēnei huarahi i te wā e mākū ana.
Go slowly and deliberately; this road is dangerous when it's wet.

Kia kaha te mahi i te rā e whiti ana.
Let's get into our work while the weather is good.

Ka ua ākuanei.
It's going to rain soon.

Ka whiti te rā, ā taihoa nei.
The sun is going to shine soon.

Ka pai anō te huarere ā tērā wiki.
The weather will be fine again next week.

Ka paki āpōpō.
It will be fine tomorrow.

Ka kaha te pupuhi a te hau.
It is going to be windy.

Ki te whiti te rā, ka haere tātou.
If it fines up, we (all of us) will go.

Ki te ua, ka kore tātou e haere.
If it rains, then we (all of us) won't go.

Kei te whiti te rā.
The sun is shining.

Kei te heke te tōtā i a au.
The sweat is dripping off me.

Kei te pararā te hau.
It's extremely windy.

Kei te hōhā au ki te ua.
I am sick of the rain.

Kei te noho au ki te kāinga, he wera rawa a waho.
I'm staying home – it's too hot outside.

Kua tōpunitia au e te ua.
I have been saturated by the rain.

Kua ū mai te hauwaho.
The east wind has arrived.

Kua mao te ua tarahī.
The light drizzle has stopped.

Kua tīhore te rangi.
It has fined up outside.

Kua māī te hau.
The wind has abated.

I rongo koe i te whatitiri?
Did you hear the thunder?

I kite koe i te uira?
Did you see the lightning?

I mākū koe i te marangai?
Did you get drenched by the heavy rain?

I te patopato te ua ki te tuanui o taku ruma.
The rain was tapping on the roof above my room.

I mīharo koe i te kaha pīataata mai o te uenuku?
Were you amazed by the glistening rainbow?

Ko Tāwhirimātea te atua o te huarere.
Tāwhirimātea is the god of the elements.

He rā pai tēnei ki te mātakitaki kiriata, hei aha te mahi!
It's a good day for watching movies – never mind work!

HUI MOTUHAKE
SPECIAL OCCASIONS

Te reo Māori is now heavily integrated in our communities across Aotearoa and its use is constantly growing and rising. This is evident at various special occasions, like prizegivings, award ceremonies, birthdays and weddings, just to name a few. In fact, it is now fairly unusual to attend an award ceremony where the presenters and recipients *don't* start with a mihi or words of acknowledgement in te reo Māori. Priests and wedding celebrants will often begin their ceremonies with words in te reo Māori as well.

So, let's take a look at some words and phrases to help us kōrero Māori at special occasions!

RĀ HURITAU
BIRTHDAYS

Birthdays should always be celebrated! An excellent excuse to get your wider family and friends together and have a party. Birthdays mark turning points in the journey of life; they are a celebration of us being here and a celebration of all our tūpuna who have gone before us. Birthdays create good memories, fun memories and they can also be reo memories!

First things first, how do we sing the famous 'Happy Birthday' song in te reo Māori?

Hari huritau	*Happy birthday*
Hari huritau ki a koe	*Happy birthday to you*
Hari huritau ki a koe	*Happy birthday to you*
Hari huritau ki a (ingoa)	*Happy birthday to (name)*
Hari huritau ki a koe	*Happy birthday to you*

Easy as, eh?! And then you can follow it up with the three cheers:

Hipi! Hipi! Hurei!	*Hip! Hip! Hooray!*
or:	
Anā hī, anā hī, anā hī, hā!	*Hip! Hip! Hooray!*

KUPU WHAI TAKE
HANDY WORDS

Huritau	*Birthday*
Perehana	*Present*
Koha	*Gift*

Keke huritau	*Birthday cake*
Pani reka	*Icing*
Wherawhera perehana	*Open presents*
Kāri	*Card*
Tunahi	*Wrap*
Whiwhi	*Receive*
Kānara	*Candle*
Poihau	*Balloon*

RERENGA WHAI TAKE
HANDY PHRASES

Mā wai tēnei perehana?
Who is this present for?

Mā wai tēnei koha?
Who is this gift for?

Mā taku tamaiti?
Is it for my child?

Mā taku tamāhine?
Is it for my daughter?

Mā taku tama?
Is it for my son?

Mā Tāmana tēnei taraka.
This truck is for Damon.

Mō Hātene ēnei hū hou.
These new shoes are for Hayden.

Mā taku kuru pounamu tēnei keke huritau.
This birthday cake is for my precious child.

Mōu tēnei poraka whutupōro.
This rugby jersey is for you.

Nā Whaea Mere i homai mō tō huritau.
Aunty Mere gave it for your birthday.

Nōu tēnei pahikara ināianei, āta tiakina!
This is your bike now, look after it!

Ko te waka tākaro tēnā a Rēweti.
That's Rēweti's toy car.

I hoatu ki a ia mō tana huritau i tērā tau.
They (singular) got given it for their birthday last year.

Nō wai te huritau o tēnei rā?
Whose birthday is it today?

Nōku!
Mine!

Nō Te Pāea!
It's Te Pāea's!

Nōna!
It's his/hers/theirs (singular)!

He aha kei roto i tēnei pouaka?
What's in this box?

He aha kei roto i tēnei mōkihi?
What's in this packet?

He aha tēnei kua tunahitia nei?
What's in this wrapping?

He perehana!
A present!

He aha ō hiahia mō tō huritau?
What do you want to do for your birthday?

He aha māu mō tō huritau?
What do you want for your birthday?

He keke me ngā kānara kei runga, he perehana hoki.
Cake with candles on it, and presents.

He perehana tino nui tēnei.
This is a huge present.

He putiputi ātaahua ēnei hei whakanui i tō huritau.
These beautiful flowers are to celebrate your birthday.

He maha ō koha huritau, nē?!
You have got heaps of birthday presents, eh?!

Me pōwhiri i a wai ki tō huritau?
Who shall we invite to your birthday?

Me haere ki hea mō tō huritau?
Where shall we go for your birthday?

Me haere ki ngā puna kaukau.
Let's go to the pools.

Me haere ki te papa tākaro mō taku huritau.
Let's go to the playground for my birthday.

Me waiata hari huritau tātou ki a Nana.
Let's sing happy birthday to Nana.

Me wherawhera perehana?
Shall we open presents?

Me pānui i te kāri i te tuatahi kia mōhio ai koe nā wai!
Read the card first so you know who it's from!

Me tīhaehae i te pepa tunahi.
Tear open the wrapping paper.

E hia ō tau?
How old are you now?

Me kaua e neke atu i te tokorima ngā hoa, nē?
No more than five friends, okay?

Me waea atu ki a Koro ki te mihi mō tāu i whiwhi ai.
You should ring up Koro to say thank you for what you received.

Kaua e wareware ki te mihi mō/i ō perehana.
Don't forget to say thank you for your presents.

Kaua e tata rawa ki ngā kānara.
Don't get too close to the candles.

Kāti te koko pani reka ki tō matimati.
Stop scooping off the icing with your finger.

Kāti te umere, tamariki mā!
Stop yelling, children!

Kaua e hauruturutu i ngā perehana, he pīrahi pea nō ētahi.
Don't shake (vigorously) the presents, some may be fragile.

Puhipuhia ngā kānara.
Blow out the candles.

Tapahia te keke.
Cut the cake.

Tohaina he keke ki tēnā, ki tēnā.
Give a piece of cake to each person.

Mukua ngā ringaringa me ngā waha.
Wipe your hands and your mouths.

Wherawherahia ō perehana.
Open your presents.

Ka kai, ka horoi utauta, kātahi ka wherawhera perehana.
We will eat, do the dishes, then open presents.

Ki te takaroa tātou, ka mahue te wā wherawhera perehana.
If we (all of us) are late, we will miss the opening of presents.

Ka toru tekau mā tahi tau koe āpōpō.
You will be 31 tomorrow.

Ka whitu ō tau ā te 17 o Paengawhāwhā.
You will be seven on the 17th of April.

Ka haere ki te huritau o Hēmi ā te ahiahi nei.
We will go to Hēmi's birthday this afternoon.

Kei te tū te huritau o Rāwiri ki te whare o tōna māmā.
Rāwiri's birthday is being held at his mother's house.

Kei te haere tāua ki te hook perehana mā Rāwiri.
We (you and I) are going to buy a present for Rāwiri.

Kei te tākaro ngā tamariki me ngā Lego hou.
The kids are playing with the new Lego.

Kei te tino harikoa ia ki tāu i hoko ai māna.
He/She is ecstatic with what you bought him/her.

Kei te haere mai koe ki te huritau o Sam?
Are you coming to Sam's birthday?

Kua hoko perehana koe māna?
Have you bought his/her/their (singular) present?

Kua mutu kē te huritau o ngā māhanga.
The twins' birthday has already finished.

Kua tekau tau koe ināianei, kei ngā whika takirua!
You are 10 now, in double figures!

Kua kite koe i te māripi koi hei tapahi i te keke?
Have you seen the sharp knife for cutting the cake?

I tunu tōtiti whero mā ngā tamariki?
Did you cook some red sausages for the kids?

I iwa tau koe i tērā tau, hei tēnei tau ka tekau koe.
You were nine last year, this year you will be ten.

I whai ia i ngā pū wai e rima.
He got (given) five water pistols.

I tonoa te whānau Tua, engari auare ake.
The Tua family was invited, but were a no-show.

I aha koe mō tō huritau?
What did you do for your birthday?

RĀ MĀRENA ME NGĀ HURITAU
WEDDINGS AND ANNIVERSARIES

Just like birthdays, weddings and anniversaries should always be celebrated! They are an opportunity to prioritise, to celebrate and to use te reo Māori, whether it be during conversations with guests and friends, or during a speech.

KUPU WHAI TAKE
HANDY WORDS

Mārena/Pākūhātanga	*Wedding*
Tūāhu	*Altar*
Taumata/Tēpu matua	*Head table*
Putiputi mārena	*Wedding bouquet*
Whakaahua	*Photo*
Taumau/Taipū	*Engaged*
Tau pūmau	*Sweetheart*
Hungarei	*Father-in-law (can be used for mother-in-law as well)*
Hungawai	*Mother-in-law (can be used for father-in-law as well)*
Taokete	*Brother-in-law of male/ Sister-in-law of female*
Hunaonga	*Son-in-law/Daughter-in-law*
Rīngi/Mōwhiti	*Ring*
Oati	*Vows*
Whare karakia	*Church*
Minita	*Priest*
Kāhui mārena	*Wedding party*
Wahine mārena/Tāne mārena	*Bride/Groom*
Pokohiwi kaha	*Maid of honour/Best man*
Kaireperepe	*In-laws*
Kaka mārena	*Wedding dress*
Kanikani tuatahi	*First dance*
Koha	*Gift*

Keke huritau	*Anniversary cake*
Kāri mārena	*Wedding card*
Huritau	*Anniversary*
Perehana	*Present*
Pō tāriana	*Stag night/party*
Pō heihei	*Hen's night/party*

RERENGA WHAI TAKE
HANDY PHRASES

Mā wai te pākūhātanga e whakarite?
Who is going to organise the wedding?

Mā te whānau o te wahine mārena te mārena e whakarite?
The bride's family will organise the wedding.

Mā wai tēnā perehana?
Who is that gift for?

Mā taku hungawai.
It is for my mother-in-law.

Mā wai te tēpu matua e manaaki?
Who will be looking after the top table?

Mā aku kaireperepe e mahi.
My in-laws will do that.

Mā te wahine mārena ēnei putiputi.
These flowers are for the bride.

Mā taku tau pūmau tēnei keke huritau.
This anniversary cake is for my sweetheart.

Mōu tēnei kaka mārena.
This wedding dress is for you.

Nā Whaea Mere i whatu.
Aunty Mere made it (the dress).

Nō wai te pākūhātanga i tēnei rā?
Whose wedding is it today?

Nō Hine rāua ko Aka!
It is Hine and Aka's!

Nōna!
It's theirs (singular)!

He aha kei roto i te whare karakia?
What's in the church?

He aha kei roto i te whare mō te ngahau?
What's in the room for the reception?

He aha tēnei kua tunahitia nei?
What's in this wrapping?

He perehana!
A present!

He aha ō hiahia mō tō mārena?
What do you want to do for your wedding?

He aha māu mō tō mārena?
What do you want for your wedding?

Kia haere ki te whare karakia, kia maha ngā putiputi, kia tokomaha ngā manuhiri, kia nui te aroha!
To go to the church, to have lots of flowers, lots of guests and lots of love!

He mōwhiti ātaahua tēnei hei whakanui i tō mārena.
This beautiful ring is to celebrate your wedding.

He maha ō koha huritau, nē?!
You have got heaps of anniversary presents, eh?!

Me pōwhiri i a wai ki tō mārena?
Who shall we invite to your wedding?

Me tū tō mārena ki hea?
Where shall we have your wedding?

Me tū ki te marae?
Shall we have it at the marae?

Me haere ki Rarotonga mō tō tāua mārena.
Let's go to Rarotonga for our (yours and my) wedding.

Me āta kōwhiri koe i tō pokohiwi kaha mō tō mārena.
Choose your maid of honour/best man carefully for your wedding.

Me kaua e neke atu i te kotahi rau manuhiri, nē?
No more than 100 guests, okay?

Me waea atu ki ō kaumātua kia haere mai rāua.
You should ring up your grandparents so they attend.

Kaua e wareware ki te mihi ki te minita.
Don't forget to say thank you to the minister.

Kaua e wareware ki ō oati.
Don't forget your vows.

Kāti te tohutohu, e Mā!
Mum, stop bossing (me) around!

Kāti te tangi!
Stop crying!

Tapahia te keke.
Cut the cake.

Tohaina he keke ki tēnā, ki tēnā.
Give a piece of cake to each person.

Mahia te kanikani tuatahi.
Time to do the first dance.

Ka hikoi taiea te kāhui mārena ki te tūāhu, ka karakia te minita, kātahi ka timata te mārena.
The wedding party will march to the altar, the minister will pray, and then the wedding will start.

Ki te takaroa tātou, ka mahue ngā oati.
If we (all of us) are late, we will miss the exchange of vows.

Ka tū te mārena ā te 18 o Maehe.
The wedding will be held on the 18th of March.

Ka haere ki te whare o te hungarei o Hēmi ā te ahiahi nei.
We will go to Hemi's father in-law's house this afternoon.

Kei te tū te pō whakanui i te mārena takatāpui nei ki te whare o Hone.
The party to celebrate this same-sex wedding will be held at Hone's house.

Kei te tū te pō tāriana o Rāwiri ki te whare o tōna taokete.
Rāwiri's stag party is being held at his brother-in-law's house.

Kei te tū te pō heihei o Hinetoa ki te whare o tōna taokete.
Hinetoa's hen's party is being held at her sister-in-law's house.

Kei te haere mai koe ki te mārena o Sam?
Are you coming to Sam's wedding?

Kua kite koe i te māripi koi hei tapahi i te keke?
Have you seen the sharp knife for cutting the cake?

I waea atu koe ki tōna hunaonga?
Did you ring his/her daughter-in-law/son-in-law?

I tonoa te whānau Horomona, engari, auare ake.
The Horomona family was invited but were a no-show.

I aha koe mō tō rā mārena?
What did you do for your wedding day?

TE AO MATIHIKO
THE DIGITAL WORLD

Te ao matihiko, the digital world, evolves at pace. It is something our tamariki have known since birth, and it's exciting to think of the innovations they'll see in their lifetime. The digital world has required innovation in terms of Māori language, too, so that we can express this fairly new element of our lives.

The great thing about Māori words is they often describe the purpose or mechanism of equipment in the name. For instance, *rorohiko* or *computer* can be broken down literally to *roro – brain*, and *hiko – electric*, which is a pretty great description of what a computer is!

KUPU WHAI TAKE
HANDY WORDS

Waea pūkoro	*Cellphone*
Waea atamai	*Smartphone*
Pūrere	*Device (generic)*
īWaea	*iPhone*

īPapa	*iPad*
īRangi	*iTunes*
Manatawa	*Android*
Rorohiko	*Computer*
Rorohiko pōnaho	*Laptop*
Papahiko	*Tablet*
Matatopa	*Drone*
Pouaka whakaata atamai	*Smart TV*
Pukamata	*Facebook*
Pae Tīhau	*Twitter*
Tīhau	*Tweet*
Paeāhua	*Instagram*
Tiki Toka	*TikTok*
Te Aka	*Vine*
Atapaki	*Snapchat*
Puahi ipo	*Tinder*
MataWā	*FaceTime*
Mataāhua	*Video call*
Pāhotanga mataora	*Stream*
Arorangi	*Live feed*
TiriAta	*YouTube*
TangiAo	*SoundCloud*
Hui topa	*Zoom*
īKiriata	*iMovie*
Matihiko	*Digital*
Hangarau	*Technology*
Ipurangi	*Internet*

Pouwhanga	*Modem*
Kupuhipa/Kupu tāuru	*Password*
Paetukutuku	*Website*
Waiwhai	*Wifi*
Pātuhi	*Text*
Tuihono	*Online*
Īmēra	*Email*
Kiriāhua/Matatahi	*Selfie*
Atakata	*Meme*
Kapua	*Cloud*
Niho kahurangi	*Bluetooth*
Whakaū/Tikiake	*Download*
Pāhorangi	*Podcast*
Rangitaki	*Blog*
Ao whakarahi	*Augmented reality*
Tuhiwaehere	*Coding*
Atamariko	*Avatar*
Mata	*Screen*
Pāwhiri	*Click*
Pūhihiko	*Charger*
Taura hiko	*Charger cord*
Rapu	*Search*
Panuku	*Scroll*
Whakaweto	*Turn off*
Miri	*Swipe*
Whakakaha/Whakahiko	*Charge (a device)*
Hōtaka-ā-tono	*TV On Demand*

Pūtea	*Credit*
Rau mahara	*USB stick*
Wheori	*Virus*
Kōtaha	*Profile*
Tohumarau	*Hashtag*
Whakahoa	*To 'friend' someone*
Wetehoa	*To 'unfriend'*
Whakaweti tāurungi	*Cyber bullying*
Haumaru-ā-ipurangi	*Cyber safety*
Taupānga/	
Pūmanawa tautono	*App*
Tohu kare-ā-roto	*Emoji*

RERENGA WHAI TAKE
HANDY PHRASES

Ko te papahiko tēnei a Mere.
This is Mere's tablet.

Nāku tēnei īWaea, nāku anō i hoko.
This is my iPhone, I bought it myself.

Nāku ēnei taupānga, waiho!
These apps are mine, leave them alone.

Nāku tēnei taura hiko?
Is this the cord to my charger?

Nā ngā tamariki katoa o tēnei whānau taua rorohiko, kei wareware i a koe.
That computer belongs to all the kids in this family, don't you forget that.

Nāu te īPapa, māu e tiaki.
It's your iPad, you look after it.

Ko ōku puru taringa/poko taringa ēnei.
These are my headphones.

Ko te rau mahara a Pāpā tēnei, ka mutu ana tāu mahi, whakahokia ki a ia.
This memory stick is Pāpā's, when you've finished your work, give it back to him.

Nō māua ko Māia te mana whakairo hinengaro mō tēnei iKiriata.
The intellectual property rights of this iMovie belong to Māia and me.

He pōturi te ipurangi ki tōku whare.
The internet is slow at my house.

He mūrere pai tēnā!
That's a good hack!

He ataoti kē tēnā, ehara i a Kanye West!
That's a hologram (over there), it's not Kanye West!

He rawe tēnei pōhi Pukamata
This is a great Facebook post.

He māmā noa iho te miri i tēnei mata, nē hā?
It's very easy to swipe this screen, isn't it?

He rāhui hangarau kei te haere ake ki te kore koutou e whakarongo mai.
There will be a ban on technology if you (three or more) don't listen.

He pūtea tāu?
Do you have any credit?

He whakahiko tāu?
Do you have a charger?

He aha te kupuhipa mō tēnei pūrere?
What's the password for this device?

He rangitaki tāna, kei te whai pūtea nui hoki!
He/She has a blog and is making lots of money too!

Kei hea te paetukutuku mō tō kura?
Where's the website for your school?

Kei hea ngā pāhorangi pukukata o te wā?
Where are the funny podcasts these days?

I TangiAo tēnei waiata.
This song was on SoundCloud.

I hea te wānanga tuhiwaehere?
Where was the coding workshop?

Kei runga i ngā hautō taku waea atamai.
My smartphone is on top of the drawers.

Kei hea aku īmēra? Auē, kua whai wheori taku rorohiko!
Where are my emails? Oh no, my computer has a virus!

Kei runga rā te matatopa, titiro!
The drone is up there, look!

Kei hea te kiore? Kāore e taea te panuku!
Where's the mouse? I can't scroll!

Kei te rārangi takaiho ngā whakamōhiotanga.
The dropdown menu is where the notifications are.

Kei ngā Hōtaka-ā-tono kē, kāore anō kia whakaū ki te
kapua.
*It's only on TV On Demand, I haven't downloaded it to the
cloud.*

Kei hea te kupuhipa mō te waiwhai.
Where's the password for the wifi?

Me whakaū i te parenga wheori ki te rorohiko pōnaho.
We should download virus protection onto the laptop.

Me ū ki tā tātou kirimana hangarau ā-whānau.
We should stick to our family digital contract.

Me whakaoti āu mahi kāinga katoa i mua i te tākaro kēmu.
You should finish all your homework before you play games.

Me mōhio a Māmā ki te kupuhipa.
Mum had better know the password!

Me noho tūmataiti tāu kōtaha Paeāhua.
Your Instagram profile should stay private.

Me whakahiko taku waea atamai, rima ōrau noa iho e toe ana.
I should charge my smartphone, it's on five per cent.

Me haukoti i ngā hokonga ki-rō-taupānga.
(You) should stop in-app purchases.

Me tango a īRangi i tana waea.
(You) should remove iTunes from his/her phone.

Me whai i te whakahounga taupānga, kua ngaro aku tohu kare-ā-roto.
I need the app update, my emojis have disappeared.

Me popore koe ki ō hoa Pukamata, pēnā i ō hoa i te ao tūturu.
You should be kind to your Facebook friends just like your friends in the real world.

Me hono tāua hei hoa Pukamata, kia kite ai au i āu pōhi.
You and I should be Facebook friends, so I can see your posts.

Me whakamahi ngā mana mātua.
We should use the parental controls.

Kaua e whakairi i taua whakaahua ki a Paeāhua.
Don't put that photo on Instagram.

Kāti te aro ki te waea.
Stop focusing on the phone.

Kaua e whāki atu i tō wāhi noho.
Don't reveal where you live.

Kaua e horokukū ki te kōrero mai mēnā kei te whakaweti tētahi i a koe.
Don't hesitate to say if someone is bullying you.

Kaua e waiho inu ki te taha o te rorohiko.
Don't leave drinks next to the computer.

Kaua e huaki i ngā īmēra paraurehe.
Don't open the junk emails.

Kāti te kohi kiriāhua ki taku waea.
Stop collecting selfies on my phone.

Kāti te whakapau i te raraunga.
Stop using up the data.

Kāti te tāhae kiriata i te ipurangi, he tāhae tonu te tāhae!
Stop stealing movies on the internet, stealing is stealing!

Kāti te tākaro, me hono kē ki a Studyladder.
Stop playing games and go into Studyladder instead.

Kāti te whakahoki kōrero ki taua tangata, he ika haehae kupenga.
Stop replying to that person, they're a troublemaker.

Kia tūpato, kaua e taka te papahiko, ka pakaru te mata!
Be careful, don't drop the tablet, the screen will break!

Kia tūpato; whakahoahoa ki ngā tāngata e mōhio ana koe.
Be careful; friend the people you know.

Kia manawanui, kāore e roa, kei a koe te wā.
Be patient, it won't be long until it's your turn.

Kia mataara, he hītinihanga kē ētahi īmēra.
Be aware, some emails are actually phishing.

Kia kaha te ako i ngā pūkenga tuhiwaehaere, ka whai hua tēnā.
Go hard to learn coding skills, that will be helpful.

Whakaweto i te īPapa!
Turn off the iPad!

Whakaitia te kahaoro.
Turn the volume down.

Waiho!
Leave it!

Whakahiko i te waea atamai.
Charge the smartphone.

Whakakorengia ēnā waiata.
Delete those songs.

Ki te pā te wheori ki te rorohiko, ka ngaro āu mahi katoa.
If a virus gets into the computer, all your work will be lost.

Ki te tūkino koe i tāu pūrere, ka ngaro i a koe.
If you mistreat your device, you'll lose it.

Ki te paki te rā, me puta ki waho, tākaro ai – hei aha te aro
ki ngā hangarau.
If the weather improves, you should go outside to play –
enough focusing on the technology.

Ka hoko pūtea anō tātou i te rā nei.
We (all of us) will get more credit today.

Ki te hurihia te tāwhakaahua, ka kite au i a koe i te MataWā.
If you turn the camera around I'll see you on FaceTime.

Ki te whakapōrearea taua tama i a koe, ka huri ki te wetehoa.
If that boy bothers you, he'll be unfriended

Ki te maha rawa aku pātuhi, ka nui rawa te nama!
If I send too many texts, my bill will be too big!

Ka whakapono au ki a koe.
I'll trust you.

Ki te pēnā koe, ka tangohia te pūrere.
If you do that, the device will get taken away.

Ki te ngaro tēnei waea, ka tere taku kimi i te ipurangi, mā te taupānga Kimihia Taku īWaea.
If I lose this phone, I would quickly look for it on the internet, using the Find My iPhone app.

Kei te mātaki whitiāhua i a TiriAta.
I'm watching videos on YouTube.

Kei te tūhono ki te ipurangi a ngā kiritata.
I'm online via the neighbour's internet.

Kei te tīni au i ngā kupuhipa katoa.
I'm changing all the passwords.

Kei te whakahoa koe ki taua ika haehae kupenga? Kia tūpato!
You're becoming friends with that troublemaker? Be careful!

Kei te rapu meka i a Kūkara.
I'm searching for facts on Google.

Kei te pau haere te kaha o te rorohiko, me whakahono i te taura hiko.
The power is running out on the computer, I need to connect the power cord.

Kei te tākaro kēmu koe, nē?
You're playing games, aren't you?

Kei te whakarite au i te hēteri. Ka pau ana te wā, ka tangi te waea, ā, kei tō tuakana te wā.
I'm setting the alarm. When time is up, the phone will beep, then it's your elder sibling's (same gender) turn.

Kei te mōhio koe me pēhea te whakahaere i tēnei pūrere?
Do you know how to work this device?

Kei te tīpako i aku hoa Pukamata.
I'm culling my Facebook friends.

Kua pau te pūmahara o taku waea, he kaha rawa nō koutou ki te whakaū taupānga.
The memory on my phone has been used up because you (three or more) upload too many apps.

Te āhua nei, me whakahou i tēnei rorohiko.
Looks like we should upgrade this computer.

Kua oti tāu mahi kāinga?
Have you finished your homework?

Tekau meneti mō te tākaro ataata, kātahi ka moe.
Ten minutes to play games, then it's sleep time.

Kua tīnihia tāu kōtaha kia tūmataiti ai?
Have you changed your profile so it's private?

Kua hōhā au ki taua kaiwhakarato ratonga ipurangi, ka kimi ratonga kē.
I've had enough of that internet service provider, I'm looking for another.

Kua pīereere te mata!
The screen is cracked!

Kua mate ki te rāhui i ngā hangarau, he haututū nō koutou.
*We've had to ban technology because you (three or more)
have been naughty.*

Kua hua mai anō aua whakatairanga hōhā!
Those annoying ads have popped up again!

Me pēhea te whakangaro atu?
How do you get rid of them?

Kua pau te wā hangarau, he wā tākaro ki waho.
Technology time is up, time to play outside.

I whakahou i aku taupānga katoa inanahi.
I updated all my apps yesterday.

I ngaro aku tuhinga nā te mea kāore au i tiaki i mua i te
paunga o te kaha!
*My documents were lost because I didn't save before the
power ran out!*

I matawai i aua kirimana.
Those contracts were scanned.

I tangi ia, he pōuri nōna ki te kōrero a tana hoa Pukamata.
*He/She cried because he/she was sad at what his/her
Facebook friend said.*

I whāngai hiko ki te īPapa i te ata nei.
I charged the iPad this morning.

I haere māua ki tātahi kia whakamahi i te matatopa.
We (he/her and I) went to the beach to use the drone.

I whakaae koe ki ngā tono tākaro kēmu?
Did you accept the game requests?

I utu koe i te nama ipurangi?
Did you pay the internet bill?

I tio te rorohiko, nā reira i mate ki te whakakā anō.
The computer froze, so I was forced to restart it.

Ka nui taku manawareka ki te auaha o tāu mahi tuhiwaehere!
I'm so pleased with the creativity in your coding work!

Hono mai ki tā mātou rōpū kōrerorero.
Join our group chat.

Puta rawa mai koutou i te kura, ka tono i ngā hangarau!
As soon as you (three or more) get out of school you want the technology!

Auē, mukua taua whakaahua!
Ew yuck, delete that photo!

Koirā te mate o taua taupānga, ka mate ki te whakahou ia rua wiki!
The problem with that app is, you have to update it every two weeks!

Me mahi Tiki Toka tāua.
Let's do a TikTok together (you and I).

I tuku atakata mai i a, titiro!
He/she sent me a meme, look!

He wāea manatawa tāna.
He/she has an Android phone.

He huitopa tā tatou āpōpō.
We (all of us) have a Zoom meeting tomorrow.

TE HĀEREERE ME NGĀ TOHU TĀWHE
TRAVEL AND DIRECTIONS

Most of us will travel from one location to another each and every day, whether it's a short journey from the *kāinga* or the home to the *toa* or the shop, or from one town to another. Giving directions in te reo Māori while travelling can be as simple as uttering just one or two words, like these:

Haere	*Go*
E tū	*Stop*
E hoki	*Go back*
E huri	*Turn*
E tuku	*Give way*
Mauī	*Left*
Matau	*Right*
Tōtika	*Straight*

Mā hea is used in conjunction with *ai* after the verb to ask how someone will be travelling. A more advanced speaker will use the first two examples (without the *ai*):

Mā hea mai koe?
How will you get here?

Mā hea atu koe?
How will you get there?

Mā hea koe haere mai ai?
How will you get here?

Mā hea koe haere atu ai?
How will you get there?

Mā hea tātou haere ai ki Te Araroa?
How are we (all of us) going to Te Araroa?

Mā runga pahi.
On the bus.

Mā hea a Hēni haere ai ki te ngahere?
How will Jane be travelling to the forest?

Mā runga waka topatopa.
In the helicopter.

Mā hea koutou hoki mai ai?
How will you (three or more) be returning?

Mā raro.
On foot (walking).

Mā raro tāua haere ai, nē?
Let's (you and I) walk, shall we?

Mā runga i tōku waka au haere atu ai.
I will travel in my own car.

The following phrases are vital if you are to arrive at your destination. If you need someone to repeat some directions, just say 'anō':

Tēnā koa.
Excuse me.

Me pēhea taku tae atu ki . . . ?
How do I get to . . . ?

Me haere tōtika.
Go straight.

Me huri mauī.
Turn left.

Me huri matau.
Turn right.

Kei hea te marae?
Where is the marae?

Kei te kokonga tuatoru, huri mauī.
At the third corner, turn left.

Kei hea a Tāmaki i tēnei mahere?
Where is Auckland on this map?

Kei hea te whare pupuri taonga?
Where is the museum?

E hia te tawhiti i konei?
How far is it from here?

E whitu kiromita.
Seven kilometres.

E hia te roa kia tae atu?
How long does it take to get there?

E rua hāora.
Two hours.

Kei te huarahi tika au ki . . . ?
Am I on the right road to . . . ?

Kei te ngaro māua.
My friend and I are lost.

Āwhina mai?
Can you help me please?

To ask the question, 'Where is the nearest . . . ?' just ask, 'Is there a . . . around here?'

He wharepaku kei konei?
Are there toilets here?

He pūrere tango moni kei konei?
Is there a money machine here?

He hereumu kei konei?
Is there a bakery here?

He kāinga taupua kei konei?
Is there a hostel here?

He papa hōpuni kei konei?
Are there any camping grounds here?

MĀ RUNGA WAKA
TRAVELLING BY CAR

Kei hea te whare kōhinu?
Where is the gas station?

Whakakīia.
Fill it up, please.

He kōhinu, he hinumata rānei?
Is it petrol or diesel?

He waka hiko tēnei?
Is this an electric car?

He whare whakahiko kei te ara/huarahi?
Is there a charging station on the way?

Horoia te mataaho.
Wash the windscreen, please.

Tirohia te hinu me te wai.
Check the oil and water, please.

Tirohia te mahere Kūkara?
Have a look on Google maps?

Whakamaua tō tātua.
Put your seatbelt on.

Āta haere.
Slow down.

He inaki waka kei te huarahi matua.
There is a traffic jam on the main road.

Whakatipihia atu!
Overtake!

Engari, kia tūpato!
But be careful!

Arotahi ki te huarahi.
Watch the road.

He motuara kei mua i a tātou!
There is a traffic island in front of us!

He huarahi kōpikopiko tēnei.
This is a winding road.

Mahia he kōnumi!
Do a U-turn!

Kei te whakapai ruaki au.
I am feeling nauseous.

Me tū tātou ki te whakatā.
Let's (all of us) stop for a rest.

He rare āu?
Have you got any lollies?

Kua tata.
Nearly there.

Kua pau te kōhinu.
It's out of gas.

Kua pau te pūhiko.
The battery is flat.

Kua pakaru te mataaho.
The windscreen is broken.

Kua pakaru te pūtororē.
The exhaust is broken.

Kua tata haukore te porotiti.
The tyre looks low.

Kua haukore te porotiti.
The tyre is flat.

I pahū tētahi mea.
Something blew up.

E kore e tukatuka.
It won't start.

Kei te pīata mai te rama hinu.
The oil light is on.

Kei te pīata mai te rama tumuringa.
The handbrake light is on.

Ki te piki puke te waka, ka pukā te pūkaha.
The engine overheats when the car climbs a hill.

MĀ RUNGA WAKA TONO
TRAVELLING BY TAXI AND UBER

Kei hea te tūnga wakatono?
Where is the taxi/Uber stand?

Kei te wātea koe?
Are you free?

E hia te utu i konei ki te tāone?
How much from here to town?

He tāhae tēnā!
What a rip-off!

Haria ahau ki te hōhipera.
Take me to the hospital.

. . . ki te hōtera Novotel.
. . . to the Novotel Hotel.

. . . ki te papa waka rererangi.
. . . to the airport.

Tatari mai i konei.
Wait (for me) here.

Tēnā koa kia tere ake.
Can you please go faster.

E tū ki konei.
Stop here.

Kei a koe te taupānga Ūpara?
Have you got the Uber app?

Tonoa he Ūpara hei kawe i a tāua.
Order an Uber to take us (you and me).

Kei te whakatata mai te Ūpara.
The Uber is getting closer.

E rua meneti ka tae te Ūpara.
The Uber will arrive in two minutes.

MĀ RUNGA WAKA TŪMATANUI
ON PUBLIC TRANSPORT

Kei hea te tūnga pahi/tereina?
Where is the bus station/bus stop/train station?

Āhea te pahi/tereina ki Kirikiriroa wehe atu ai?
When does the bus/train to Hamilton depart?

Ā te toru, te whā me te rima karaka.
At three, four and five o'clock.

Āhea te pahi/tereina tae atu ai ki Te Whanganui-a-Tara?
When does the bus/train arrive in Wellington?

Āpōpō.
Tomorrow.

E hia ōna tūnga?
How many stops does it make?

Ka tū ki hea?
Where are the stops?

E hia te utu mō ngā tīkiti?
How much are the tickets?

E rima tāra, e whā tekau heneti.
$5.40.

E hia te roa o te haere?
How long will the trip take?

E ono hāora.
Six hours.

Tēnā koa, homai he hōtaka pahi/tereina?
Can I have a bus/train schedule, please?

He pahi hōpara kei konei?
Is there a sightseeing tour bus?

Ka haere te pahi hōpara ki hea?
Where does the sightseeing tour bus go to?

Āhea te pahi e whai ake nei?
When is the next bus?

Tīkiti ahutahi, koa.
One-way ticket, please.

Tīkiti takaāwhio, koa.
Return/Round-trip ticket, please.

Ko tēhea te pahi ki . . . ?
Which bus goes to . . . ?

Ki hea au makere atu ai?
Where do I get off?

Ki te tūnga e whai ake nei.
At the next stop.

E haere ana tēnei pahi ki tō māua hōtera?
Is this bus going to our (two) hotel?

MĀ RUNGA WAKA RERERANGI
TRAVELLING BY PLANE

Me whakarerekē/whakakore au i taku tīkiti.
I want to change/cancel my ticket.

He utu tāpiri mō tērā?
Is there an additional cost for that?

Kia rua tūru mōku i te waka rererangi ki . . .
I would like two seats on the plane to . . .

Āhea te wā whakaturuma?
What time is check-in?

Āhea rere ai?
What time does it depart?

Āhea tau ai?
What time does it land?

Ko te whitu karaka i te pō te wā tatū.
The arrival time is 7 p.m.

Ko te ono karaka i te ata te wā o tō rerenga.
Your flight is at 6 a.m.

Ko te toru karaka i te ahiahi te wā wehe.
Departure time is 3 p.m.

Kei hea te tomokanga mō te waka rererangi ki . . . ?
Where is the gate for the plane going to . . . ?

He aha te nama o te waka rererangi?
What is the flight number?

He waka rererangi auahi kore tēnei.
This is a smoke-free flight.

He iti rawa ō Pirorere.
You have insufficient Airpoints.

He taumaha rawa tō pēke.
Your bag is too heavy.

Me haere ki te wāhi whakataka pēke.
Go to the bag drop.

Me hari ō tīkiti whakaeke.
Take your boarding passes.

Kei te Koru?
Where is the Koru Lounge?

He inu māku.
Can I have a drink?

He heihei māku.
I'll have the chicken.

He mīti kau māku.
I'll have the beef.

Kāore au i te hiakai.
I am not hungry.

He aupuru anō mōku, koa?
Can I have another pillow, please?

He paraikete anō mōna, koa?
Can he/she have another blanket, please?

Kaua e whakaoho i a au mō te kai.
Please don't wake me for a meal.

Kaua e tuku i tō tūru kia tītaha muri mai!
Don't put your seat back!

Kaua e hoihoi!
Stop being so noisy!

Kaua e oma!
Don't run!

Kaua e tū, kei te kori tonu te waka!
Don't stand up, the plane is still moving!

Kaua e ngaro tō puka uruwhenua!
Don't lose your passport!

Kia pai tō rere!
Have a nice flight!

INGOA WĀHI
PLACE NAMES

The Māori term for the naming of places and landmarks is called *tapa whenua*. There were many ways our people came up with these names, including the following examples:

- Transplanting ancestral names and symbolism from eastern Polynesia to New Zealand places (e.g. *Rarotonga* is the name for the area in Auckland now known as Mt Smart; the many instances of *Hikurangi* names across the country).
- Taunaha (naming after body parts) to emphasise personal claims to land (e.g. *ihu* for nose; *takapū* for stomach).
- Naming places according to their physical or geographical features.
- Naming places after people.
- Naming for historical or spiritual reasons (e.g. voyaging).
- Naming to celebrate cultural icons (e.g. Kupe, Māui).

The next time you come across a Māori place name, see if it contains any of the following words in it, which can give you a clue to its meaning:

Ao – cloud
Aotearoa (roa = long, tea = white, ao = cloud)

Puke – hill
Pukekohe (a hill that was intensely populated by kohe trees in former times)

Puna – spring
Taka**puna** (taka = assemble, puna = spring; some of the first arrivals to the area gathered at this spring to quench their thirst)

Maunga – mountain
Maungawhau (maunga = mountain, whau = the whau plant, aka cork tree, that grew in abundance on the mountain)

Wai – water
Waimakariri (wai = water, makariri = cold)

Whanga – bay
Whangamatā (whanga = bay/harbour, matā = obsidian)

In recent times, there has been a significant effort made across many sectors in New Zealand society to correctly pronounce Māori place names and to include the original name for places in Aotearoa. This improved effort has been especially noticeable on our broadcasting platforms like radio, television, social media, and especially in weather forecasts. Correct pronunciation of Māori names, in my opinion, shows an immediate indication of respect and value towards the language and the culture, which is appreciated by Māori. The key, of course, to correct pronunciation is the vowel sounds, which we covered at the beginning of this book. However, in addition to having a focus on getting the vowel sounds right, there are also a couple of other tips I can offer you.

Firstly, make sure that you check whether there are macrons present on the name. It is reasonable easy to test this by using the many online te reo Māori dictionaries that are available. Some will even come with an audio pronunciation guide.

The second point is where to put the emphasis. In the English language, the emphasis generally falls on the middle syllables or part of the name – think about, for example, Wellington, Ashburton or Cambridge. In the Māori language, the emphasis generally lands on the first syllable or part of the name, for example, Rotorua, Taihape and Waitangi. This is especially so when there is a macron on that first syllable or part of the name, such as Rāwene, Ōtautahi and Tāmaki Makaurau.

Macrons will generally demand some form of emphasis wherever they are positioned in the name. This emphasis happens naturally when correct pronunciation takes place because you must elongate the vowel sound – a versus ā (aa), e versus ē (ee), i versus ī (ii), o versus ō (oo) and u versus ū (uu). When pronouncing the place name Taupō, for example, the emphasis will be where the macron is sitting.

Here are some similar examples: Whangamatā, Whangārei and Ngāruawāhia (emphasis where both macrons are). Try to avoid putting a macron on a word that does not have one! The prime example of this happening is in the pronunciation of one of the Māori names for the South Island – Te Wai Pounamu. As you can see, there is no macron present; however, there are many of us who 'invent' a macron on the 'a' in the last word, and therefore incorrectly pronounce the name as Te Wai Pounāmu!

Take a look at the following list of common place names in Aotearoa and have a go at saying them, using the information we have just discussed about emphasis and macron placement to help you. Let's start at the tail of the fish of Māui and progress to the head, then cross Raukawa Moana Cook Strait to Te Wai Pounamu!

TE IKA A MĀUI
THE NORTH ISLAND

Whangārei – Emphasise the macron ā part of this name and remember you are getting off easy on this one because the full name is Whangārei Terenga Parāoa, or the gathering place of whales, as named by local iwi Ngāti Wai. Another well-known version of the name is Te Whanga-ā-Reipae, or the waiting place of the ancestress Reipae. Local iwi include Ngāti Wai, Ngare Raumati, Ngāi Tāhuhu and Te Parawhau.

Tāmaki Makaurau – Again, emphasise the macron ā part of this name and let the rest flow nice and evenly off the tongue. There are many versions regarding the origin of the name but most agree that it is a metaphor alluding to the many resources and fertile areas of the region, and therefore desired by and sought after many – and so, Tāmaki of a hundred lovers. Local iwi include Ngāti Whātua Ōrākei, Tainui, Te Wai-o-Hua, Ngāi Tai, Ngāti Pāoa, Marutūahu and Te Kawerau-a-Maki.

Kirikiriroa – No macrons here and it's a name that should have an even flow from start to finish. If you have difficulty, try breaking it into the two words that make up the name – *Kirikiri* and then *roa*. Also, focus on the i vowel sound, as in e̲vil. Kirikiriroa means a long stretch of gravel – *roa* means long, *kirikiri* means gravel. It refers to a stretch of the Waikato River where the current town of Hamilton sits. The local iwi is Waikato Tainui.

Tauranga – The full name is actually Tauranga Moana. Again, there are no macrons so no need to elongate any vowel sounds. There may be some emphasis on the *Tau* part of the word. The *nga* sound should the same as singer, not finger. A *tauranga* is a resting place or a place for safe anchorage – hence the name Tauranga Moana. Local iwi include Ngāi Te Rangi, Ngāti Pūkenga, Waitaha and Ngāti Ranginui.

Rotorua – This is the short form of the beautiful name Te Rotorua-nui-a-Kahumatamomoe or the Great Lake of the ancestor Kahumatamomoe. It was discovered and named by Kahumatamomoe's nephew Īhenga. A *roto* is a lake; the *rua* is two or second. This is because it was the second lake of the area discovered by Īhenga. Perhaps the most difficult part of pronouncing this name is the r sound, similar to the double d part of the word shudder. The local iwi of the city area is Ngāti Whakaue.

Ahuriri – This is the Māori name for Napier. It is said to be named after a great chief called Te Ahuriri who resided in the area and had a huge influence on creating lagoons and waterways, to take advantage of the ocean's bountiful resources. Remember, more emphasis on the *Ahu* than any other part of the name. Napier is the domain of Ngāti Kahungunu.

Ngā Motu – Ngā Motu is the name of the area most will refer to as New Plymouth, and it means the islands. Ngā Motu was the name of the Māori hapū that lived around Paritūtū and, when under threat or duress, out on the islands, especially Motumāhanga. The elongated sound where the macron is placed and having accurate vowel sounds are the key to pronouncing this name correctly. This is an area where Taranaki iwi hold mana whenua.

Te Papaioea – Te Papaioea was the original name given to Palmerston North by early Māori, meaning 'how beautiful it is'. This was in reference to the location of the settlement next to the Manawatū River. It can be quite a difficult name to say if you are not a speaker of te reo Māori, especially the *ioea* part. My advice would be to take your time saying that part and really be conscious of what those vowels should sound like, maybe practising your *a-e-i-o-u* beforehand! Rangitāne is the local iwi.

Taranaki – This is a name that unfortunately is commonly butchered! There needs to be the rolling Māori r sound on the first part of the word, and be very aware to not be influenced by the Pākehā term 'the Nacky' when pronouncing the second part! Mt Taranaki will be officially known by its pre-European title, Taranaki Maunga, in the near future. It will lose forever the name of Egmont, bestowed on it by Captain James Cook in honour of a British earl who never stepped foot in Aotearoa. I believe the park, which the maunga dominates, will also lose its connection to English aristocracy – Egmont National Park will soon be officially known as Te Papakura o Taranaki. Obviously, Taranaki iwi are the local people.

Whanganui – Is it Whanganui or Wanganui? This is a question I get asked a lot! The city's spelling was corrected to Whanganui in 2017, which in te reo Māori can be interpreted as 'big bay' or 'big harbour'. It was originally misspelled because of the local dialect and the almost undetectable *h* in the digraph *wh*. When the people of this area say words like *whānau*, it sounds like *wānau*. Likewise, *Whanganui* sounds like *Wanganui*. My advice to people is that if you are from the area and speak the local dialect or want to acknowledge the local dialect, then you will pronounce it *Wanganui*. If you are from outside the area and don't speak the local dialect, then the 'f' sound on *Whanganui* is fine. Some of the local tribes include Te Atihaunui-a-Pāpārangi, Ngāti Hauā and Whanganui.

Te Whanganui-a-Tara – This is the name given to the Wellington harbour. Whatonga was the captain of the *Kurahaupō* waka, which is said to have had a tumultuous journey across the Pacific from eastern Polynesia, eventually landing at Nukutaurua on the Māhia Peninsula. He had two sons, Tara and Tautoki, who settled in the Wellington area and the top of the South Island. Tara is immortalised in the name of the Wellington harbour, used today for the central Wellington area and city. Another name is Te Upoko-o-te-Ika, or 'the head of the fish', demonstrating Māori people's ability to 'view from the heavens' and identify the shape of the North Island as a large whai, or stingray. This is also why, in te reo Māori, we would say going 'up' to Wellington – *Kei te piki au ki Te Whanganui-a-Tara* – and 'down' to Kaitāia – *Kei te heke au ki Kaitāia*. This is a good example of the difference between a Māori worldview and a Pākehā worldview. Local iwi include Taranaki Whānui and Te Ātiawa.

TE WAI POUNAMU
THE SOUTH ISLAND

Whakatū – The Māori name for Nelson means 'to construct or establish'. This is reasonably easy to pronounce – just make sure you let the name flow evenly with perhaps a slight emphasis on the 'tū'. The wh sound is like an 'f' in English. There are eight tribes recognised in the area – Ngāti Kuia, Ngāti Apa ki te Rā Tō, Rangitāne, Ngāti Toa Rangatira, Ngāti Kōata, Ngāti Tama, Ngāti Rārua and Te Ātiawa.

Ōtautahi – This is the generally accepted name for Christchurch but there is debate about it. One version of the name recounts an ancestral village on the banks of the Avon River called Ōtautahi. Another version talks about a Ngāi Tahu chief named Tautahi, who serves as the origin of the name. When saying Ōtautahi, keep the emphasis at the front of the word, especially on the 'Ō'. Try not to say the second syllable of the word, i.e. *tau* like the first part of '<u>tow</u>er'. *Tau* should sound like the toe on your foot. Local iwi include Ngāi Tahu.

Kawatiri – This is the name commonly used for Westport but is the actual name of the Buller River. Kawatiri means 'deep and swift' in te reo Māori. Usually, I would advise the t sound in the word Kawatiri to sound almost the same as a soft 'd'. The main iwi on the West Coast are Ngāi Tahu and Kāti Māmoe.

Māwhera – The Māori name for Greymouth originates from an ancient pā or village in the area, called Māwhera. The name of the pā itself was taken from the river Māwheranui, which means 'to be open or widespread'. When using the Māori name, remember the emphasis will be on the *Mā* part of the word.

Piopiotahi – A beautiful Māori name for what we now call Milford Sound. One story talks about a (now extinct) bird called a piopio accompanying legendary hero Māui on his mission to win immortality for his beloved people. Māui perished and his companion the piopio was said to have flown to Piopiotahi in mourning. Split the word into two parts when pronouncing it – *Piopio* and then *tahi*. The vowel sounds are also key to correct pronunciation of this name – as they always are! Local iwi include Ngāi Tahu and Kāti Māmoe.

Ōtepoti – The original name for the wider area is Ōtākou, after a Ngāi Tahu village near the head of the harbour that bears the same name. The area at the top of the harbour where Dunedin began to be developed is where the Ōtepoti settlement lies and is said to refer to the place where canoes landed. Ngāi Tahu holds mana whenua in the area.

Rakiura – The name for Stewart Island. It is said to refer to the glowing skies or the famous southern lights. *Raki* (or *Rangi*) is the sky and *ura* means to glow. The local iwi include Ngāi Tahu.

NGĀ KĪWAHA
IDIOMS AND SLANG

Māori speakers love using idioms, colloquialisms and slang. This, however, can be problematic for someone new to the Māori language, because these expressions usually have a specialised meaning known only by the group of people or tribe that created them. New idioms and colloquial expressions are being created every day. They are symbolic of conversational language, representing both figurative thinking and fun, and to some degree indicate the health and vitality of a language. They generally have a figurative meaning completely separate from the literal meaning or definition of the words, leaving most of us scratching our heads and wondering, *What on earth did he or she mean by that?!*

Take the well-known Māori-language expression from the Taranaki region: 'Whano, kia motu te taka o te roi!' This basically means: 'Take no prisoners!' (A pretty common statement heard in any sporting arena, for instance.) Now, if I was to literally translate this expression – 'Go forth and cut (motu) the tap root (taka) of the fern root (roi)' – would you still be able to ascertain its true meaning? Or, if you are being completely honest with yourself, are you now thinking it should relate to gardening? This is the beauty of idiom to the native or fluent speaker, and the difficulty of idiom to the newcomer or language learner.

Let's look at another example, but this time from the English language: 'It's raining cats and dogs.' If I were to utter this particular idiom to someone who knew very little English, they would probably look to the sky and wait for this miraculous event to happen. So, I would have to explain to this person that 'raining cats and dogs' figuratively means that it is raining very heavily. The following phrases are one-off sentences for you to use while you are speaking Māori to someone. As I mentioned earlier, they may have been understood by only the group or tribe who first uttered them originally, but have since become part of everyday Māori language.

Meinga! Meinga!
Is that so!?

Tō ihu!
Butt out!

Nā whai anō.
Well that explains it.

Ākene koe i a au!
You watch it or else!

Nā wai tāu?
Says who?

Kāore i a au te tikanga.
My hands are tied.

Nāwai rā, nāwai rā.
Eventually.

Āe mārika!
For sure!

Hoihoi koe!
Bite your tongue!

Anā e pūkana mai nā.
Right under your nose.

Ki konā koe mate kanehe ai?
Are you lovesick or what?

Kāore e kore.
Without a doubt.

Hei aha atu māku?!
Why should I care?!

E rua, e rua!
Two of a kind!

Kāti i konei!
This ends here!

Pakaru mai te haunga!
How terribly offensive!

Ka kino kē koe!
You're too much!

Te tū mai hoki o te ihu.
What a snob.

Kua mau tō iro?
Have you learnt your lesson?

Ka tau kē!
Fantastic!

He kōrero i pahawa.
All talk, no action.

Kaitoa!
Serves you right!

Ehara, ehara.
On the contrary.

Nō hea te ūpoko māro e aro.
He's too stubborn to understand.

Nā wai hoki tātou i a koe!
Look what you've got us into!

Ko wai koe?
Who do you think you are?

Ka kai koe i tō tūtae!
You will regret it!

Parahutihuti ana te haere!
Couldn't see them for dust!

Mā tēnā ka aha?
What difference will that make?

Nāna anō tōna mate i kimi.
She thought she knew better.

Puku ana te rae!
He hit the roof!

I reira te mahi a te tangata!
The place was packed!

Kei noho koe!
Don't even think about it!

Kaikainga ngā taringa.
Got an earful.

Engari tonu.
You bet. / For sure.

He aha hoki!
No way!

Aua atu.
Don't worry.

Kua taka te kapa.
I get the picture.

Hei aha māu!
Mind your own business!

Me karawhiu!
Give it heaps!

He rā nō te pakiwaru!
Very hot day!

Mā te aha i tēnā.
Better than not at all.

Me hāngai te kōrero!
Don't beat around the bush!

Āmiki rawa tēnā!
Too much information!

Pōuri atu!
Make way, I'm coming through!

Engari koe!
Gee, you're the man!

Koia kei a koe!
You're awesome!

Nāia!
Here it is! / Here you go!

Kātahi rā hoki!
How astonishing (good or bad)!

I wāna nei hoki!
Poor thing!

Ka aroha kē!
How sad!

Mō taku hē!
I'm sorry!

Nē?
Is that so? / Really?

E kī rā?
Is that so? / You don't say?

Te anuanu hoki!
Whoa, that's disgusting/ugly!

Kei konā au!
I'm with you on that!

Hoea tō waka!
Off you go! / You're on your own!

Kia ahatia!
So! / So what!

Kāti te patu taringa!
Stop battering my ears!

Kāti te horihori!
Stop telling lies!

Koia! Koia!
That explains it!

Koirā anake te mahi e pahawa i a koe!
That's all you're good for!

Kua oti te ao!
That says it all!

Koinā tāku!
That's what I reckon/think!

Kua riro māna ināianei.
The ball's in his court now.

Auare ake.
To no avail.

Tē taea e rātou!
They haven't got a chance!

Te hiapai hoki!
What a damn cheek!

Mā koutou anō koutou e kuhu!
You can fend for yourselves!

Mea ko au koe . . .
If I were you . . .

Ka patu tōna pīkaru.
Fast asleep. / Out to it.

Hika mā!
For crying out loud!

Tōna tikanga.
Supposedly.

Kotahi atu.
Make a beeline for.

Whakaputa mōhio!
Know-it-all!

Kāore e nama te kōrero.
Has an answer for everything.

Te weriweri rā!
That creep!

Tuhia ki tō rae.
Never ever forget it.

Kātahi te whakaaro pōhēhē ko tēnā!
What a daft thought!

Kei tāwauwau kē koe!
You are way off track!

Kāore he painga i a ia!
No sweat to him/her!

Kua hiki te kohu?
Get the picture?

Mea rawa ake . . .
Next minute . . .

Manohi anō.
On the other hand.

Kua kino kē ngā piropiro.
In a foul mood.

Hanepī tonu atu.
Dumbfounded.

Hau pirau!
Exaggerating! / Laying it on thick!

Ka kari tonu!
Still digging/persisting!

Kua tangi kurī.
Crying for nothing.

Whakangaro atu koe!
Get lost!

Kua pakaru te pūkoro!
Broke (no money)!

Taputapu kē!
Neat! / Choice! / Cool!

Ka mātua i tēnā!
That'll do!

Ehara i te tī!
You only live once!

Ka mau te wehi!
That's amazing!

Karawhiua!
Give it heaps!

Kua pau te hau!
I'm absolutely stuffed/exhausted!

Taku matakawa atu.
I hated/hate it.

Pakaru ana te tangi.
Cried his/her eyes out.

Tē mōhio hoki.
No idea whatsoever.

Tau kē!
Excellent!

Autaia!
Pretty good!

Te āhua nei.
It looks that way. / It looks like it.

Hurō!
Hooray!

He taringa kōhatu.
Deaf ears. / Never listens.

Autaia tonu.
Not bad.

TE AO MĀORI

THE MĀORI WORLD

TIKANGA
MĀORI PRINCIPLES
AND VALUES

Māori principles and values are guided by what is known as *tikanga*. This is an ancient term used to describe a set of guidelines that underpin how to interact, how to behave (i.e., what is the right way and what is a trespass) and how to conduct specific cultural traditions, such as pōwhiri. Being familiar with and understanding tikanga Māori will help you during all manner of interpersonal interactions, whether it be one on one, in public occasions, when dealing with Māori entities and whānau, or in business. This includes basic things like performing a simple *karakia* or incantation at the start of meetings, knowing how to deliver a *mihi* or words of acknowledgement in te reo Māori, knowing how to do the *hongi* or pressing of noses in greeting (and understanding its significance), and taking shoes off before entering a home or a particular room or building.

Let's take a look at the components of the pōwhiri to ease you into it.

NGĀ PŌWHIRI
FORMAL WELCOMING CEREMONIES

A formal welcoming ceremony on a marae, in the workplace or in any other arena is called a *pōwhiri*. A shorter and less formal version of a pōwhiri is sometimes called a *whakatau*. There are tribal variations to this process, so enquiring beforehand about the local tikanga should always be your first port of call!

REO

Usually, Māori language only is spoken. It is a Māori context, after all, and no apology should be made for this. Some marae and workplaces may change this on special occasions, and say some words in English, but this isn't typical. They may also provide space during the pōwhiri process for high-ranking people, both male and female, to speak. The local people will dictate how this happens. The language you hear generally follows a pattern, so you may be able to glean some understanding if you recognise these patterns. I will discuss the patterns used in the explanations around *karanga* and *whaikōrero*.

KARANGA

The *karanga* or ceremonial call is usually performed by the women to begin the formal welcome. If you are in the northern parts of the country, don't be too surprised if a male responds to the karanga! When you hear the women begin to call, this is your cue to start moving forward on to the marae, or towards wherever your gathering is being held. An expert at performing the karanga will take years to perfect the art. Women who perform karanga are held in high esteem by the tribe. The roles of men and women in the pōwhiri ceremony are equal and complementary, not discriminatory – which, unfortunately, is a common interpretation by those viewing the process through the lens of the Western world. There have been instances where non-Māori women have felt belittled and upset when they are asked to sit on the seats behind the male speakers. Women are, in fact, the first speakers in this process. They can set the agenda, express opinions and make relevant statements during their karanga. You will sometimes hear women telling the men what to say, if they are in close enough proximity, and some will even stand and start singing to sit the man down if he is waffling, being incoherent or saying outrageous things! Karanga are almost always performed at pōwhiri but may not be performed during the less formal whakatau. At a whakatau, you may be just ushered in to where the welcome will take place.

What is the pattern most karanga follow? Here is an example.

Karanga whakaeke – Call to enter

Nau mai, haere mai ki runga i te papa tapu e hora nei.
Welcome, enter on to the sacred ground beneath us.

Haere mai, haere mai!
Welcome, welcome!

Be ready to recognise the words 'haere mai' or 'nau mai'. These are the words that are saying 'Welcome here today' as well as saying 'Come towards me / Start to walk this way'.

Karanga hunga mate – Acknowledge those who have passed on

Mauria mai rā ō koutou mate.
Bring forth the memories of those who have passed.

Utaina mai rā hei tīpare mō ngā poroporoaki a te iwi e.
Assemble them together as a wreath for the laments of the people.

Haere e ngā mate, haere, haere, haere atu rā.
So that we can once again bid them farewell.

At this point, be ready to recognise words such as mate (the deceased), poroporoaki (farewell) and the phrase 'Haere, haere, haere atu rā', which means 'Go forth (the deceased) on your journey to eternity'.

Karanga hunga ora – Secondary call to the living

Whakatata mai rā e ngā manuhiri whakahirahira, haere mai rā ki tā tātou kaupapa whakawhanake pakihi.
Approach, my valued visitors, welcome to our gathering to discuss the development of our business.

Haere mai, haere mai, haere mai rā!
Welcome, welcome, welcome!

Māori custom stipulates that after farewelling the deceased, you must return the focus of your words to those who reside in the physical realm. Keep an ear out for the word 'manuhiri' (visitors) and phrases like 'Hoki mai rā ki a tātou' (I now return my thoughts back to us (the living)), 'te hunga ora' (the living), 'kaupapa o te rā' (theme of the day), and a repeat of 'Haere mai, haere mai, haere mai' (welcome once again, welcome to you all).

WAEREA

Waerea are a type of karakia or incantation a male will perform in unison with the karanga to ward off any negative influences that may be present during the pōwhiri. They are incantations to protect the visiting group and ensure safety. They are not commonly heard but are very beautiful and add layers to the sounds you will hear when you are entering on to the marae or to the location where your hui is being held. Waerea are usually only performed when you are visiting a place for the first time, not when you are on a return visit.

WERO

Most people will assign the term 'challenge' to describe the *wero* but it is so much more than that. In the old days, it was a demonstration of a tribe's prowess with weaponry, a demonstration of the power and prestige of the local people. It was used to ascertain the intention of a visiting group of people and whether their purpose was one of peace or warfare. If it was for the latter reason, the warriors performing the wero may take a few of the visiting tribe out before returning to the safety of the fortifications to prepare for full-scale war. If they were coming in peace, the visitors would be disarmed as they entered the fortified part of the village. They would enter one by one through a very small entrance to ensure a mass attack couldn't occur. The wero is now very much a ceremonial part of the pōwhiri process. The ethos behind it, however, remains the same – a demonstration of the power and prestige of the local people. Wero are usually performed only at very important occasions and pōwhiri. They are not performed at the less formal whakatau.

KARAKIA

Karakia is quite difficult to define, but perhaps the closest translation is 'incantation'. There are many different types of karakia such as *atahu* (love charms), *kawa* (to remove tapu from a new building), *tohi* (baptism), *pure* (purification), and *whakanoa* (to remove tapu – see page 195). In the workplace, karakia are used to start and end formal meetings (see pages 59 and 64), to start and end the workday, to bless food, and sometimes, on a deeper level, to purify and bless the workstation of a staff member who has passed on.

In a pōwhiri setting, a karakia is sometimes performed before the start of the speeches. Once you have reached your seating area, it's okay to take your cues from your hosts as to whether to sit down right away or remain standing. Just look across and make a 'shall we sit down?' motion or action. They may tell you to remain standing because they are going to perform a karakia before the speeches start. This happens on some marae, schools and workplaces. It can be a little bit embarrassing when you go to your seating area, sit down, and then your hosts tell you stand back up for the karakia, or you may feel a little bit awkward during the karakia because you are sitting down while others are still standing! The karakia performed may be Māori in origin with incantations, or Christian in origin where there will be prayers. It's a bit hit-and-miss as to whether a karakia will happen, be it pōwhiri or whakatau, so just be aware!

WHAIKŌRERO

Whaikōrero, or oratory, is an artform that expresses flair, drama, charisma and the wealth of traditional knowledge the speaker has acquired during their lifetime. It is very impressive to watch when performed by an expert. There are two whaikōrero protocols: *tāutuutu*, which is when the speakers from both sides alternate; and *pāeke*, which is when all the host speakers will speak first, then all the visitor speakers will follow. Again, if you are speaking but are unsure what the protocol is, make a 'shall I get up now?' gesture to the other side; they will either nod or make a 'no, not yet!' gesture.

As with karanga, there is a general pattern to whaikōrero. Most speakers will follow this general pattern or format, but this can vary, and will depend on the expertise of the speaker and the occasion. See page 68 for step-by-step information to help you build your own generic whaikōrero.

Okay, now let's take a look at what the pattern of whaikōrero looks like (you will notice the language of whaikōrero is much more metaphorical than everyday language!).

He whakaohooho – Evocation

Ka tangi te tītī.
The sooty shearwater calls.

Ka tangi te kākā.
The kākā calls.

Ka tangi hoki ko au.
I call in unison.

Tihei mauri ora!
And exhort the breath of life!

This is the part that sounds like the speaker is rapping! It has a flow, a beat, and the words sound like they are coming out really fast! Some speakers will perform this part of their speech with a lot of gusto to gain the attention of the audience. Listen out for the 'Tihei mauri ora!' (I exhort the breath of life!) line.

Mihi mate – Acknowledge those who have passed on

Tuatahi, ki ngā raukura o te mate kua maunu atu ki moana uriuri.
First and foremost, I pay homage to the plumes who have drifted to the foreboding ocean

Haere atu rā koutou.
Farewell to you all.

You may recognise this part when the mood of the speaker changes and they may take on a more sombre tone. If that doesn't happen, words such as *mate* (deceased), *poroporoaki* (farewell) and the phrase, 'Haere, haere, haere atu rā', which means 'Go forth (the deceased) on your journey to eternity', should tip you off that the speaker is now acknowledging those who have passed on.

Mihi manuhiri – Welcome to visitors

E ngā hau e whā o te motu.
To the tribes from the four winds.

Piki mai, kake mai!
Welcome on board!

Just like the karanga, when performing the whaikōrero, our Māori customs stipulate that after farewelling the deceased you must return the focus of your words to those who reside in the world of the living. Again, keep an ear out for the word 'manuhiri' (visitors) and phrases like 'Hoki mai rā ki a tātou' (I now return my thoughts back to us (the living), 'te hunga ora' (the living), 'kaupapa o te rā' (theme of the day), and 'Haere mai, haere mai, haere mai' or 'Nau mai, piki mai, kake mai', which are variations of 'Welcome once again, welcome to you all'.

Mihi i te kaupapa – Acknowledge the theme of the day

He rā whakahirahira tēnei he rā harikoa hoki mō tātou katoa.
This is indeed a special and joyous occasion for us all.

Koinei te rā e whakanui ai tātou i te huritau rima tekau o Mere!
This is the day when we celebrate Mary's 50th birthday!

Nō reira, e Mere, ngā manaakitanga a te whānau ki a koe.
Therefore, Mere, we the family wish you all the best.

This part may be difficult to understand because the language used will be relevant to whatever the occasion might be. In this example, the occasion is a birthday. Listen for words like *kaupapa* (the theme or reason), *whakahirahira* (special) and *harikoa* (joyous).

Whakatepe – Conclusion

E te iwi, kia ngahau tātou, engari me tiaki tātou i a tātou.
All those in attendance, let's celebrate, but remember to look after each other.

Tēnā koutou, tēnā koutou, tēnā tātou katoa.
Greetings to us all.

Concluding comments are usually preceded by a 'Nō reira', which kind of means 'Therefore/and so'. You may also hear something like 'Me mutu i konei' (I shall finish here). You will know when the speech has reached its end when you hear 'Tēnā koutou, tēnā koutou, tēnā tātou katoa' or 'Greetings once again, to all of us gathered here today'.

WAIATA

It is expected that each speaker will perform a *waiata* or song to conclude their speech in the appropriate way. This is called a *whakarehu* and symbolically releases the speaker from the transcendental position they were in as they performed their whaikōrero. This is because the speaker assumes an important position and will often recite ancient knowledge and history of a very sacred nature during their speech, thereby causing their personal tapu levels to rise. A waiata is sung after the speech to bring these levels back to normal. At the conclusion of the waiata, the speaker should sit down; no concluding comments are necessary unless very, very short; if the speaker continues at length after the waiata, they would need to sing again! The other function of the waiata is to support what the speaker has said. The waiata is generally selected because it matches the sentiment in the speech. At the conclusion of the waiata, if you have stood up to support, you may sit back down. There is no need to keep standing, even if the speaker continues on!

KOHA

Traditionally, a koha was a gift of food or a precious treasure. Nowadays, it is money. Koha is under the jurisdiction of a custom called *utu* or reciprocity. What is given is expected to be returned at some stage, but it may be generations later before the gift is reciprocated. Some events might ask for a koha rather than a set admission fee.

In a pōwhiri, the gifting of a koha usually occurs at the end of the waiata. The speaker (often the last of the visiting speakers to speak) will place a gift or donation on the ground. They will take a few steps forward, usually to about halfway between where the host and visiting speakers are seated, and carefully place the koha there. The speaker then will take a few steps back, turn to their right, and return to their seat. The hosts receiving the koha will do the same – usually, but not necessarily, offering some words of gratitude as they pick up the koha.

HONGI AND HARIRŪ

When Māori greet one another by pressing noses, the tradition of sharing the breath of life is considered to have come directly from the gods.

Māori folklore recounts the story of the first human, a woman, being created by the gods by moulding her shape out of the earth. All of the gods made their own contributions to the creation of this form. Tāwhirimātea, the god of the winds, designed and placed the lungs and breathing apparatus into the shape; Tūmatauenga, the god of warfare, created the muscles, tendons, cartilage and sinew; Tūkapua, the god of the clouds, supplied the whites of the eyes, and so it goes on. When the form had been completed, it was the famous god Tāne who embraced the figure, placed his nose on hers and transferred the breath of life into her nostrils. She then sneezed and came to life. Her name was Hineahuone or 'the earth-formed woman', and she is widely accepted as being the first human being.

When performing the *hongi*, you are paying homage to the creation of the first human, Hineahuone, and all your ancestors who descend from her to you. You are also paying homage to the descent lines of the person you are performing the hongi with. The *hā*, or the breath of life, is exchanged and intermingled. A lot of people are apprehensive about performing the hongi. The best way to approach it is to let the other person guide you. Some people will press noses twice, others just once. Some will inhale quite deeply when your noses touch, others will hold their nose to yours for quite a long time. Just go with it!

Here are some tips to get you through this process:

- If you are in a 'hongi line', watch the person in front of you and see what the 'hongi technique' is of the next person you are going to hongi with.
- Place your left hand on their right shoulder – this helps you to guide them so you don't smash heads, miss each other's noses or end up kissing!
- Relax, it's what we do, so go for it – and if it doesn't work out, have a laugh about it!

KAI

Food or *kai* after the pōwhiri or whakatau is an important part of the process. Cooked food is seen as a potent negator of tapu, and since you have just been in a very tapu process, i.e., the pōwhiri, food afterwards will return your tapu levels to normality. This potent power of cooked food is the reason why things like passing food over a person's head (the most tapu part of the body) is a big no-no in Māori culture. Other things to be aware of are not sitting on tables, and not mixing items related to clothing with food; for example, not putting hats, glasses and items of clothing on the table.

NGĀ TIKANGA MĀORI
CUSTOMARY CONCEPTS

Hopefully, from the pōwhiri process, you have begun to see that tikanga is informed by ancient knowledge that essentially protects us and helps organise ideas into action.

Here are a few more important values, principles and customary concepts that are part of tikanga Māori.

MANA

This word is commonly used by the general population because it sums up so many different things – authority, control, force, power, prestige, influence, to name a few. It is impossible to provide a single English word that accurately describes mana. I guess its multiple meanings is why so many people love the word and use it on a regular basis! Mana is generally bestowed on a person by others in recognition of that person's skill, achievements or actions. Mana gives a person the authority to make decisions, to lead an initiative or group, to organise. Depending on the person's performance and success, mana can increase or decrease. Remember, the source of all mana comes from our gods, so mana carries a huge expectation of respect and regard. Humans are the agent of mana, but never the source.

TAPU

Mana goes hand in hand with *tapu*: one affects the other. The more prestigious and reputable the person, the object (for example, a carving) or the event, the more it is surrounded by tapu and mana. Tapu generally translates to sacred or forbidden. A special ceremony using traditional incantations would need to be performed to lift a tapu and make things *noa* or normal again. Tapu is always present but increases or decreases depending on the situation. For example, when a person is sick, their tapu increases, causing some restrictions to be put on them such as quarantine, until they get well again and their personal tapu returns to a normal level. Tapu is intrinsic and can be used to set limits and boundaries.

MAURI

Mauri is general described as life force, vitality or energy. Mauri, like tapu, is intrinsically linked to mana. Without the presence of mauri, mana cannot accumulate and flourish in a person or object. All things in the physical world are said to have mauri. Sometimes, it is a person's mauri that is affected by sickness or mākutu (see page 199). The mauri of a place can be affected too, creating a negative or unenviable state. Things like pollution affect the mauri of a place.

MANAAKITANGA

This generally translates to showing respect and care for others. It also speaks to humility and kindness to make any place a positive and conducive environment that fosters good relationships. Māori place high value on manaakitanga, whether at a whānau or tribal level. Even if someone arrives unannounced at your house, a high level of manaakitanga is expected to be shown. This will usually take the form of food but also showing warmth and hospitality to whoever your guests may be and using te reo Māori where possible. Manaakitanga can be the source of mana, another very highly valued principle in the Māori world.

WHANAUNGATANGA

This principle relates to kinship and building positive relationships with others, no matter what positions they hold and no matter what their status is. It encourages collaboration and teamwork to achieve results, but also encourages people to feel like a whānau! It is a unifying force, creating cohesion and buy-in towards the achievement of common goals. In my opinion, this is the key principle that determines the success and well-being of any team, whānau, workplace or community. When positive relationships or whanaungatanga are built, success is inevitable!

KAITIAKITANGA

This is a concept used by many to connect and engage with the environment. It encourages best practice to maintain and protect the natural resources being used. It can, however, be adapted to include things like the protection of equipment and the well-being of family and friends. Kaitiakitanga can apply on an individual level also. Anybody can demonstrate personal kaitiakitanga by looking after their own health and well-being – physically, mentally, emotionally and spiritually – so that they can make greater and more meaningful contributions at work, in the community and at home. Their individual kaitiakitanga then has a positive impact on the kaitiakitanga of all.

RANGATIRATANGA

This principle speaks about leadership and the demonstration of leadership qualities. Things like humility, showing respect, understanding the holistic culture that guides Māori people's thought processes and being mindful of cultural awareness of things like pronouncing a person's name properly and not sitting on food tables. (A quick aside, the reason why sitting on tables is not the done thing is that tikanga Māori keeps the tapu, or sacredness, of the body well away from the *noa*, or non-sacredness, of food. As with most tikanga, it's also pretty much common sense and hygiene – do we really want to eat something from where a kumu has been?)

WHAKAPAPA

The recitation of whakapapa or genealogy is a high artform as well as being a miraculous feat of memory. Whakapapa experts are able to recite hundreds of names in proper order stretching back to the beginning of time. Therefore, whakapapa is not just about human genealogies; it is also a metaphor for the evolution of the universe and the creation of the world and all living creatures within it. It provides meaningful links between humans and the environment. In terms of whakapapa, Māori regard themselves as the younger siblings of the trees, birds, fish and just about all creatures created by the gods, before the god Tāne created the human race. Māori people are expected to relate and react respectfully towards the environment because of this. Unfortunately, in today's society, this is not always the case! The art of reciting whakapapa is still practised but the names and the histories that flesh out the genealogies are nowadays also committed to paper and recorded digitally. To know your ancestry is very important in Māori culture.

MĀKUTU

This used to be a powerful force in traditional Māori society and acted like a disciplinary law to maintain order. Most people will translate *mākutu* as witchcraft or sorcery, but, as with most things pertaining to Māori religion and spirituality, it has a much deeper and more multifaceted meaning than that. In today's society, there are still many instances where a person's ill health or unusual behaviour is attributed to mākutu. A person affected by mākutu can exhibit a decline in energy, mental capacity and health. Very particular rites need to be carried out by a qualified and ratified tribal expert to cure a person of this type of affliction.

TANGIHANGA

If someone says they are going to a tangi or tangihanga, they are going to a funeral. Traditionally, a Māori funeral would last several days and sometimes weeks. The body was wrapped in harakeke (flax) and kawakawa leaves and smeared with kōkōwai or red ochre. It was adorned with feathers of rank and either propped up or laid on a bundle of mangemange (fern). Nowadays, the *tūpāpaku* (body of the deceased) is kept on the marae, usually in an open casket, and dressed in fine ceremonial clothes. Speeches are delivered directly to the tūpāpaku as the *wairua* (spirit) is yet to depart to the abode of eternity. Māori believe the tūpāpaku should never be left alone, so the *kiri mate* (deceased's immediate family), and particularly the women of the local tribe, will keep constant vigil over the tūpāpaku until it is taken to the *urupā* (burial ground) for interment. You are expected to attend the tangi if you knew the deceased. With some preparation, a visit to a marae for a tangi can be a very purifying experience and a chance to say goodbye to a loved one.

HĀKARI

Especially after attending a tangihanga or funeral, you will be invited to partake in the *hākari* or feast. There are many types of hākari – those that are held to celebrate an event, those that are held for religious or tikanga reasons, and those that are held to mark birth, marriage or death. Hākari are important for many reasons. They strengthen whanaungatanga or relationships, and they are an opportunity for the local tribe to demonstrate their manaakitanga or hospitality and to serve up the local delicacies. They are also important in terms of normalising levels of tapu, especially after a tangihanga or important meeting. Yes, we don't just have a 'feed' because we are good at it and like eating! There is actually a deeper meaning to it. If we take the context of tangihanga as an example, the rites and processes around the deceased are very carefully handled, and coming into contact with these processes and, indeed, the deceased person themselves, heightens the levels of tapu surrounding you. Food, as mentioned previously, is a powerful negator of tapu, so to partake in the hākari and consume cooked food is seen as a way of returning you to normality and neutralising the tapu that was around you during your experience of tangihanga.

HAKA

Haka was, and still is, a very important feature of Māori life. It is an iconic symbol of Aotearoa New Zealand on the world stage and, along with te reo Māori, differentiates us from other people in the world. Haka is a vigorous, energetic challenge performed by both men and women depending on what particular type of haka is being executed. The messages in haka can vary – sometimes they are political, sometimes they recount history, sometimes they are encouraging people to demonstrate particular personal or tribal characteristics. The widening of the eyes is called *pūkana*, the protruding tongue is called *whētero*. (Only men perform whētero due to their 'equipment' below the waistline; another explanation for whētero is the tongue as the vehicle to express sentiment via words.)

As we all know, the champion All Blacks rugby team performs the haka. The 'Ka Mate' haka is well known throughout the world and is a strong symbol of the indigenous Māori culture of Aotearoa New Zealand. Composed by Ngāti Toa Rangatira Chief Te Rauparaha in the 1820s, 'Ka Mate' encapsulates some of the themes of war: uncertainty, life, death, escape and heroism.

According to tradition, Te Rauparaha was being pursued by war parties from the tribes of Ngāti Maniapoto and Ngāti Tūwharetoa: their wish was to exact revenge on Te Rauparaha for having suffered defeat at his hands some years before. Te Rauparaha fled to the western shores of Lake Taupō and asked local chief Te Wharerangi for protection. Te Wharerangi permitted Te Rauparaha to hide in a kūmara pit. He then asked his wife Te Rangikoaea to sit over the pit. This was done because of the neutralising effect that she, as a woman, had on various incantations. As the pursuing enemies entered the village of Te Wharerangi, they were heard chanting their incantations. Te Rauparaha felt sure he was doomed and muttered the words, 'Ka mate, ka mate! (I die, I die!)' He heard one of his pursuers, Tauteka, asking Te Wharerangi where he was. Te Wharerangi replied that Te Rauparaha had long gone, heading south towards Rangipō. He uttered the words, 'Ka ora, ka ora! (I live, I live!)' Tauteka and his men were not convinced, however, and Te Rauparaha gloomily said again, 'Ka mate, ka mate!' Eventually, they were persuaded by Te Wharerangi (said to be a hairy man, hence the reference to a 'tangata pūhuruhuru' in the words of the haka) to head towards Taranaki where Te Rauparaha would undoubtedly seek refuge, and so Te Rauparaha whispered, 'Ka ora, ka ora! Tēnei te tangata pūhuruhuru nāna nei te tiki mai i whakawhiti te rā (I live, I live! For this is the hairy man who has fetched the sun and caused it to shine on me again)'. As his pursuers left the village of Te Wharerangi, Te Rauparaha emerged from the kūmara pit. As he climbed out, he said, 'Upane, upane! Upane, ka upane whiti te rā! (I take my steps out to freedom, to where the sun shines on me once again!)'. According to ancient accounts, after emerging from the pit, Te Rauparaha then performed his famous haka to Te Wharerangi, Te Rangikoaea and the rest of the village.

Ka mate, ka mate	*'Tis death, 'tis death*
Ka ora, ka ora	*'Tis life, 'tis life*
Ka mate, ka mate	*'Tis death, 'tis death*
Ka ora, ka ora	*'Tis life, 'tis life*
Tēnei te tangata pūhuruhuru	*Behold! There stands the hairy man*
Nāna nei i te tiki mai whakawhiti te rā	*Who will cause the sun to shine*
Upane! Upane!	*One upward step! Another upward step!*
Upane! Ka upane!	*One last upward step! Then step forth!*
Whiti te rā!	*Into the sun, the sun that shines!*

TANIWHA

Māori legends contain many stories of encounters with *taniwha* (water-dwelling spirits), some friendly, some not so friendly! There have been many occasions when taniwha and the strong belief in them has disrupted work or construction. Many taniwha are seen as kaitiaki or guardians of a particular place and can be appeased by having meaningful and respectful dialogue with the local tribes about the best way to proceed. A good example of this came in 2002 when Ngāti Naho, a tribe who live in the Meremere area north of Waikato, successfully lobbied to have part of State Highway 1 rerouted in order to protect the dwelling of their legendary kaitiaki who would appear as a large white eel. Transit New Zealand and Ngāti Naho discussed the matter and work was put on hold. Ngāti Naho insisted the taniwha must not be removed because to remove the taniwha would be to invite trouble. Local tohunga or traditional spiritual leaders eventually appeased the taniwha, and concessions were made to move the road to not disturb the abode of the taniwha.

TĀ I TE KAWA

People are generally fascinated by opening ceremonies but always ask the question, 'Why do we have to get up at four o'clock in the morning?!' Opening ceremonies performed under Māori protocols and karakia are becoming more and more frequent. I have opened many new buildings and occasions in the past few years, from new gyms, to new premises of well-known businesses, to new police stations, to art exhibitions – you name it! This type of ceremony is called *tā i te kawa*, literally 'to strike with a branch of kawakawa'. In traditional times, this was a ceremony carried out in connection with the opening of a new carved house or the launching of a new canoe. It is still performed today in contemporary settings to imbue positive energy and vitality into a building, bringing it to life. The building is named, and it becomes a safe haven for all those who dwell in it or use it. The ceremony is always carried out pre-dawn – not always at 4 a.m.; it might be 5 a.m., depending on the time of year! The reason for this is that according to Māori spiritual beliefs, pre-dawn is the time when traditional Māori gods are at their most powerful and most potent. It is the best time to call on them to send forth their mana. The concluding incantations coincide with the rising of the sun, welcoming a new day, a new beginning, a new building.

TE TIRITI O WAITANGI
THE TREATY OF WAITANGI

The Treaty of Waitangi has been, and most likely will always be, a point of discussion and debate, so it can be tricky to fully ascertain how it applies to our everyday lives. Everybody loves having the day off work on Waitangi Day, but what does it all mean? Let's begin with a brief background.

HE WHAKATAKI POTO
A BRIEF HISTORY

Aotearoa New Zealand was largely a Māori world right up until the 1830s, which, when you think about it, isn't that long ago! There were more than 100,000 Māori, living as tribes, throughout the country. Māori language was the medium of communication in all aspects of social, commercial and political life. Māori customs, language and social structures continued to prevail, even as Europeans arrived in New Zealand. Europeans numbered about 200 in the North Island in the early 1830s. By 1839, those numbers had grown to around 2000 throughout the country (1400 in the North Island).

Eventually, the numbers of European settlers in Aotearoa New Zealand grew and the English language began to take hold.

As I explained in more detail in the introduction (see page 11), the word used to translate the concept of sovereignty was at the last minute changed from *mana motuhake* to *kāwanatanga* – an amendment that would have a major impact in the Treaty's interpretation and application for decades to come.

Regardless, on 6 February 1840, or *te tuaono o Huitanguru 1840*, is the day we can say gave birth to our nation as we know it today. The Treaty was signed by 43 chiefs gathered in a tent made from ships' sails and erected outside James Busby's house on the Treaty Grounds at Waitangi. After each chief signed, William Hobson would proclaim 'We are one people' – '*He iwi tahi tātou.*' (He would have had to say that 43 times!)

The Treaty is generally recognised as our founding document and there are two versions – one in Māori and one in English. Māori are termed 'Tāngata Whenua', the indigenous signatories; anyone else in the country is termed 'Tāngata Tiriti', signatory partners. This is where Pākehā, Chinese, Pacific Islanders, Italians, Brazilians and any other ethnic groups sit. International law says if a treaty is signed between two nations, the indigenous version must take precedent.

In a nutshell, the Treaty of Waitangi consists of:

Article 1 – Māori give the Crown *kāwanatanga* or the right to govern New Zealand citizens; both Māori and any other ethnicity living here.

Article 2 – Māori retain their sovereignty (translated in the Treaty as *tino rangatiratanga*) over all their valued possessions, both tangible and intangible (so this might include things like land, fisheries, the haka and te reo Māori).

Article 3 – Both partners, Tāngata Whenua and Tāngata Tiriti, have equal rights in this country.

NGĀ MĀTĀPONO
PRINCIPLES

In 1989, the Department of Justice pinpointed five principles of the Treaty to help organisations, businesses, government departments and individuals to understand the objectives and essence of the document. These have since been condensed into three guiding principles: **partnership**, **participation** and **protection**. These principles are quite controversial in themselves, as many Māori academics and experts feel that they tend to 'water down' the true spirit and meaning of the Treaty.

Considering many of the younger generation who are working now were not taught about the Treaty at school, it's not surprising that our interpretations of its relevance are varied. Yet, around the world, our Treaty is considered, by indigenous people especially, to be a fascinating living document that has contributed hugely to the unique fabric of Aotearoa New Zealand.

WHY TREATY PRINCIPLES MATTER

Why recognise the Treaty and how do we put its principles into action?

Whether you realise it or not, the Treaty permeates many facets of our lives. There is guaranteed Māori representation in Parliament – currently seven seats – and there is a strong push for this to also be the case on our local councils. The Māori economy's net worth is estimated to be in excess of $80 billion, with tribal and Māori business wealth growing exponentially each year. The Waitangi Tribunal still has some 300 claims to hear, most of them about land, but there are others about health, water, and coastal areas. These decisions will impact us all. Māori have major control and assets in some of our core industries such as farming, forestry and fisheries. Māori language has been one of our two official languages since 1987 (alongside New Zealand

Sign Language) – English is not official *in legislation*, but is the language of the majority, so is official by default!

You will hear Māori being spoken more and more regularly. Some companies, such as TVNZ and Air New Zealand, have strong language programmes in place already which they are benefiting from immensely. So, let's take another quick look at the main principles and how we might apply them:

Partnership

Application of this principle could include strategies that encourage working together with Māori on community projects and decisions. Engaging with the local Māori community, hapū and iwi to explore Māori concepts is hugely rewarding and enriching.

Participation

Application of this principle would be similar to that of the principle of partnership, that is, to encourage and/or strategise meaningful dialogue and relationships with Māori so that they have respected input into decisions that affect them and their whānau within the wider community.

Protection

Application of this principle could include fostering and encouraging the use of te reo Māori by using basic greetings and recognising traditional and new Māori names for places and spaces. You could research some *uara Māori* or Māori values to help guide behaviour and expectations in your everyday life.

The goal of these principles is to make sure Māori people and whānau are treated equally and that Māori values, language and culture protected in the Treaty are respected and encouraged by all.

IMPLEMENTING THE TREATY

What do you need to do if your goal is to implement the Treaty of Waitangi as part of the day-to-day life in your whānau? Here are some suggestions.

1. Study up on the Treaty

Unfortunately, our education system has been remiss in teaching New Zealand's history, so to ensure you and those around you have a clear understanding of the Treaty, I recommend diving in and reading, listening and watching heaps of quality material about the Treaty.

2. Identify who the local hapū and iwi are in your region

If you don't have a relationship with the local hapū/iwi, then create one. Most iwi will have liaison people who will be able to help and facilitate. The benefits of creating a good, strong, reciprocal relationship with tāngata whenua are hugely positive – the tribe could become good friends of yours and maybe do things like provide you with their marae as a venue for your family's significant events.

3. Make the Treaty visible in your home

Hang a copy of the Treaty on a wall in your house. You could also represent this partnership in artwork or other creative and decorative ways.

4. Utilise Māori values and concepts

Use some of the whakataukī or proverbs in this book to inform new projects and behaviours in your whānau. Give pets and other things a Māori name.

5. Normalise te reo Māori around the home

Create bilingual signage in the house using the terminology in this book. Make it normal for Māori to be heard and spoken. Use it in emails and when you greet someone. Welcome them to your home with a hearty 'Haere mai!' Focus on pronunciation too! Correct pronunciation of greetings and names goes a long way in recognising and respecting the language, the culture and its people. This book is designed to help you implement this.

MATARIKI

Ahakoa te nuinga o te motu ka whakanui i a Matariki hei tohu i te tau hou Māori, te tau hou Aotearoa, ko ngā iwi o te uru, ka whakanui kē i a Puanga. It is important to note at the beginning of our discussion about the star cluster of Matariki, also known as Pleiades, that even though most of the country celebrate Matariki as the symbol of the Māori New Year (or as I like to say, New Zealand's New Year!), the tribes of the west and some in the north celebrate the star Puanga, or Rigel, as the beginning of the New Year.

Matariki has gained in popularity over the past few years, thanks in no small way to the efforts of Dr Rangi Mātāmua, who was named Kiwibank New Zealander of the Year in 2023. It was also timely that we had Dame Jacinda Ardern in place as a prime minister who fully supported Matariki becoming a public holiday in 2022, a demonstration of the value and respect she has for Māori knowledge and Māori culture.

It is important to understand how the Māori calendar works to know exactly when Matariki rises and signifies the beginning of the New Year, because it is based on a lunar calendar that changes slightly year by year. However, it usually occurs around the months of June and July. It is based on what is called a heliacal rise; this is when a star or planet is seen on the eastern horizon just before the rising of the sun. In Aotearoa, Matariki disappears at the beginning of winter because of its close proximity to the sun, and then Matariki 'returns' and becomes visible again in midwinter. This heliacal rise of Matariki in midwinter indicates the arrival of the New Year.

There are many different interpretations of Matariki and its origins. One talks of Matariki being 'Ngā mata o te ariki Tāwhirimātea' – the eyes of the deity, Tāwhirimātea.

To cut a long story short, in the beginning of time, the primeval parents Ranginui (sky father) and Papatūānuku (earth mother) clung together in a marital embrace and produced some 70-plus children. Eventually, these children became unhappy with their living arrangements between their parents – no light and no room – so they came together to discuss how they might alleviate their plight. To do this, they developed a language of communication, the early beginnings of te reo Māori. They also developed some protocols when they met that are still the basis for how Māori conduct hui. Eventually, they decided to separate their parents and this was achieved by one of the children, Tāne.

Tāwhirimātea, god of the winds, was enraged. He did not agree with the parents being separated and, in his fury, gouged out his own eyes and threw them towards the chest of Ranginui. His eyes splintered in the sky and formed the star cluster Matariki. This is why Tāwhirimātea is a blind god who demonstrates no prejudice when causing chaos and destruction to all in his path. Matariki is a time of reflection, of remembrance, of looking to the future, and of celebration.

NGĀ WHETŪ O MATARIKI
THE STARS OF MATARIKI

There are many tribal variations on how many stars are observed, acknowledged, and celebrated during the rising of Matariki. Let's take a look at nine of them and what they symbolise.

Matariki – known as the mother of the eight stars in the cluster. Matariki is connected to health and well-being and is often viewed as a sign of good fortune or health to come in the following year.

Pōhutukawa – the eldest of the sibling stars. Pōhutukawa is connected to the dead and those who have passed away in the preceding year. This is a female star.

Tupuānuku – the star associated with food that is grown in the ground. Incantations are made to her to ensure that crops and food supplies flourish. This is a female star.

Tupuārangi – associated with food that comes from the sky and is linked to birds like the kererū and elevated foods, such as berries and fruits. This is a male star.

Waitī – connected to fresh water and living creatures in the rivers, streams and lakes. This is a female star.

Waitā – said by some to be the twin brother of Waitī. This star is associated with the ocean and all the food gathered from the sea and is also significant for its influence over tides.

Waipuna-ā-rangi – a female star connected to the rain. The name translates to 'water that pools in the sky'.

Ururangi – a male star connected to the wind. The name itself means 'the winds of the sky'.

Hiwa-i-te-rangi – the youngest of the cluster, this female star is commonly called the wishing star. Traditionally, Māori would use this star to set their desires and dreams for the year, or what we now call New Year resolutions. These hopes and aspirations are usually environmentally based – for example, for a prosperous season and a healthy taiao, or natural world. They may also request the continued health and well-being of the people and the tribe. So no, you can't ask for the Lotto numbers – it doesn't work that way!

TE KIMI I A MATARIKI
HOW TO FIND MATARIKI

Here are my four easy steps to find Matariki when it rises in the midwinter months of June and July.

1. Look towards the eastern horizon before the sun rises, so get up early e hoa mā!
2. Look for three bright stars in a line. This is Tautoru, or Orion's Belt.
3. Start to track your eye line to the left of Tautoru until you come to a group of stars that look like a triangle or a pyramid; this is the face of the bull – Taurus, or Te Kokotā.
4. Keep moving your eye line slightly to the left of Te Kokotā and there you should see the cluster of Matariki.

KUPU WHAI TAKE
HANDY WORDS

Rangi	*Sky*
Pōuri	*Dark*
Kāhui	*Cluster*
Whetū	*Star*
Whetūrere	*Comet*
Matakōkiri	*Meteor*
Matariki	*Pleiades*
Puanga	*Rigel*

Atutahi	*Canopus*
Whānui	*Vega*
Pīataata/Tīramarama	*Twinkle*
Titiro ake	*Look up*
Marama	*Moon*
Aorangi	*Planet*
Karakia	*Incantation*
Hākari	*Feast*
Hautapu	*Traditional Matariki ceremony*
Umu kohukohu whetū	*Oven to cook food offerings for the stars of Matariki*
Te Mātahi o te Tau	*The New Year*
Maramataka Māori	*The Māori lunar calendar*

HE WHAKATAUKĪ MATARIKI
MATARIKI PROVERBS

These proverbs are handy to use in conversations about Matariki or at Matariki time, and also to write on cards and gifts during celebrations of Matariki:

1. Ka mahi ngā kanohi tīkonga o Matariki.
    *The ever alert and protruding eyes of Matariki –
    alluding to being awake and alert at night-time.*

2. Matariki Tāpuapua.
   *The pools of Matariki – referring to the time of the
   year and the rain that falls, creating pools of water on
   the ground.*
3. Ka puta Matariki, ka rere Whānui, ko te tohu o te tau.
   *Matariki appers and Whānui flees – signalling the
   New Year.*
4. Te ope o te rua Matariki.
   *The company of the cavern of Matariki – used for
   the many chiefs who have departed to the cavern of
   Matariki, but is also used for the living, when a group
   of high-ranking people gather in one place.*
5. Matariki hunga nui.
   *Matariki, the gatherer of people – people gather
   together for Matariki festivals and celebrations,
   therefore Matariki unifies and bonds us.*
6. Kua haehae ngā hihi o Matariki.
   *The rays of Matariki are widespread – there are
   many stories and values associated with Matariki,
   encouraging people to share stories, reflect on the
   past and plan for the future.*
7. Ka mahuta ake a Matariki i te pae, ka mahuta ake ngā
   tūmanako mō te tau.
   *When Matariki rises above the horizon, our
   aspirations rise for the year ahead.*

HE KĪANGA MATARIKI
MATARIKI PHRASES

Ko Matariki te tohu o te tau hōu.
Matariki indicates the New Year.

Titiro ki tērā whetū.
Look at that star.

He pō pai tēnei mō te mātai whetū.
This is a good night for stargazing.

Kei te kite koe i a Matariki?
Can you see Matariki?

He uaua te kite i a Matariki.
It's difficult to see Matariki.

Kei kora!
It's there!

Kei te mauī o Te Kokotā.
It's to the left of the Te Kokotā cluster.

He aha ngā kōrero mō Matariki?
What are the stories about Matariki?

E hia ngā whetū o te kahui o Matariki?
How many stars are in the Matariki cluster?

Me haere tatou ki te hautapu o te hapori.
Let's go to the local Matariki ceremony.

Kei hea tērā?
Where is that?

Kei te maunga o . . .
It's at . . . mountain.

Me haere ki tētahi wāhi, he pōuri te rangi.
Go to a place where the sky is dark.

Ka tino kite koe i a Matariki.
You will clearly see Matariki.

Āhea te hararei mō Matariki i tēnei tau?
When is the Matariki holiday this year?

Tirohia te maramataka Māori?
Have a look at the Māori lunar calendar.

Mānawatia a Matariki!
Celebrate Matariki! (Also used as a Matariki greeting or farewell.)

HE WHAKATEPE
AFTERWORD

Remember, every time you use te reo Māori, whether it be individual words or small phrases, you are making a positive contribution to the normalisation and continued survival of our country's native language. There are many languages across the world that are on the brink of extinction but, here in Aotearoa, we have the opportunity to foster positive attitudes and goodwill to a language that gives us our international point of difference and identity.

Be strong and determined – kia kaha, kia manawanui – on your language journey. Start small with achievable goals. Find some friends and whānau to join you on the te reo Māori waka; connect with them and create environments where you can practise your pronunciation and your te reo expertise on each other. Always look for the next challenge or the next new thing you can learn. But most of all – have heaps of fun!

PENGUIN

UK | USA | Canada | Ireland | Australia
India | New Zealand | South Africa | China

Penguin is an imprint of the Penguin Random House group of companies, whose
addresses can be found at global.penguinrandomhouse.com.

Penguin
Random House
New Zealand

First published by Penguin Random House New Zealand, 2024

10 9 8 7 6 5 4 3 2 1

Text © Meka Media, 2024

Design by Cat Taylor © Penguin Random House New Zealand
Author photo by Carolyn Sylvester © Penguin Random House New Zealand
Prepress by Soar Communications Group
Printed and bound in Australia by Griffin Press, an Accredited ISO AS/NZS 14001
Environmental Management Systems Printer

A catalogue record for this book is available from the National Library of New Zealand.

ISBN 978-1-77695-075-1
ISBN 978-1-77695-897-9 (audio)
eISBN 978-1-77695-396-7

penguin.co.nz

MIX
Paper | Supporting
responsible forestry
FSC
www.fsc.org
FSC® C018684